RUNES GUIDEBOOK

Bianca Luna

Cover art: Raffaele De Angelis
Internal art: Cosimo Musio
Graphic layout: Lo Scarabeo

© Lo Scarabeo 2011

Lo Scarabeo
Via Cigna 110, 10155 - Torino, Italy
Tel: 011 283793 - Fax: 011 280756
E-mail: info@loscarabeo.com
Internet: http://www.loscarabeo.com

Printed by CT Printing

First Italian edition: September 2011
First English edition: June 2012

RUNES GUIDEBOOK

by Bianca Luna

TABLE OF CONTENTS

RUNE INDEX

INTRODUCTION

Prior to writing this book, I sat down on my sofa, took a deep breath, lit a stick of incense, and tried to relax as much as possible, emptying my mind of the usual thoughts and worries.

I own numerous sets of runes in different forms (wood, stone, and crystal), which I have either purchased over the years, have been given, or, in some cases, I have personally created. When I finally felt calm and at peace, I took the bags containing my many sets of runes and tipped them onto the table, taking time to touch and observe the stones.

The question I wished to pose to this ancient oracle was this: what should my frame of mind be in order to undertake the writing of this book? This was a period in my life when I was feeling lazy and distracted, and as I wished to question the oracle regarding such an important project, I decided that the runes incised onto black agate stone would be perfect. In the tradition of crystal therapy, this stone represents trust, concentration, and the capacity for self-regeneration. I discarded the runes I would not use and concentrated on the black agate, slowly rolling the bag in my hand while concentrating on the questions I wanted to ask. Finally, with my eyes closed, I extracted a single rune from the bag: Laguz, which is associated with intuition and femininity.

How was I supposed to interpret this rune? What did it want to tell me? I let my mind roam and slowly, everything became clear.

Laguz was telling me to let go and that perhaps my laziness in beginning writing was hiding nothing less than a resistance; in other words, a fear.

A fear of what? It wasn't necessary to answer that question immediately, but I wondered if it could be related to the fear of not being capable of working on the project. In order to confirm my theory, I extracted another rune: Algiz, long connected to energy and success. Great! The rune had reassured me in part; enough to no longer think about my fears. I returned once more to my original question, again concentrating on the Laguz rune.

As I mentioned before, this rune is connected to the principles of femininity and intuition, as well as receptiveness and heat. It seemed natural for me to interpret this meaning as advice about the writing: in composing the content of this book I needed to use a personal and direct style—nothing too complicated or formal. My job was to bring the runes to life as a tool that could be used every day. Satisfied with the answers given to me by the runes, I placed them in their bag, turned on the computer, and began to write.

Bianca Luna was born in the small town of Casterino, located in Valley of the Marvels, under the sign of Pisces. She developed an interest in astrology, tarot, runes, and other occult subjects at an early age. Bianca lives in a small house in the middle of the mountains where she writes books, tends an organic vegetable garden, and raises brigasca sheep. She gives seminars on evolutionary magic throughout Europe.

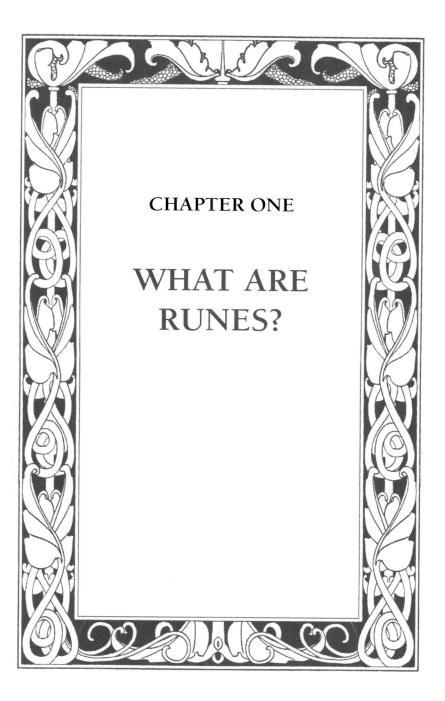

CHAPTER ONE

WHAT ARE RUNES?

Before entering into the mystical realm of the energies and powers of the runes, it is necessary to review the history of these stones in order to better understand where they come from and what they represent. They have an ancient history, intricate and mysterious, which originates in the Nordic and Germanic regions. Over time, the runes have evolved and been modified, but they have always maintained their spiritual force, and it is this force that arrives into our hands when we use them. Let's take a trip back in time to discover the roots and the history of this powerful and fascinating oracle.

THE RUNIC ALPHABET

The word alphabet comes from the ancient Greek, from the sequence of the first two letters that it composes: alpha and beta. Ancient Germanic populations, who wrote the runes, however, used the Futhark alphabet instead of the Greek. Futhark was nothing more than a runic alphabet whose name was derived from the sequence of the first six runes that it made up: Fehu, Uruz, Thurisaz, Ansuz, Raidho, and Kenaz.

Each rune corresponds to a sign, and each sign corresponds to a sound, exactly like our alphabet. The oldest Futhark we are aware of dates back to the fifth century A.D. and is made up of twenty-four runes.

Over the centuries, the runes have undergone modifications. In some cases, such as in the Anglo-Saxon tradition, the runes were initially made up of twenty-eight runes and were then increased to thirty-three. In other cases, the number of runes was reduced, such as in the case of the Armenian tradition (eighteen runes) and the Norrena tradition (sixteen runes), which dates from the ninth century A.D.

As you can see, runes have a very complex history. The runes are something vital and subject to changes and modifications, just like language. They remained an integral part of life for the Nordic populations until the 1800s when Swedish farmers began displaying them as protective talismans on the front of their homes.

THE ETYMOLOGY OF THE WORD RUNE

In each of the Germanic languages, the word *rune* means "mystery and secret." These concepts—mystery and secret—have also remained as meanings or nuances in many words of modern Germanic languages.

For example, the archaic English verb *to rown* means "to whisper or to talk under one's breath." In German, *raunen* means "to murmur," and in German Swiss, the word *ran* indicates "a secret agreement."

Let's take a step back: the word rune signifies mystery and the sequence of the runes composes an alphabet. That alphabet serves to make words, which in turn makes phrases that illustrate concepts and facilitate knowledge. The runes, therefore, lead to a secret knowledge and an esoteric teaching spoken in a low voice, whispered and hushed, from the masters into the attentive ears of the disciples.

RUNIC HISTORY

The origins of the runes are ancient, and appear uncertain and confusing today. Their existence is verified in ancient archeological findings and on objects of various origins that have been inscribed with runic signs.

As we know very little about the birth of this alphabet, the debate surrounding the runes is still open in many cases. For example, some experts identify the helmet of Negau as being the first Runic finding. It was discovered in Slovenia and dates from 400 B.C. It has an inscription that is thought to be an archaic version of the Futhark. Not everyone agrees with this interpretation. Other experts believe the inscription is in the Etruscan alphabet, which precedes the Runic alphabet.

Another ancient Runic finding is the Meldorf Fibula, discovered in Jutland in Denmark and is from the year 50 B.C. More Runic finds have appeared as particular stones: the Dolmen Tombs, which date from the prehistoric megalithic period and are made up of two or more standing stones mounted onto a horizontal stone; and the Menhir-Great Stones, which are rectangular-shaped and function as indicators of sacred sites. Examples of Menhir-Great Stones can be found in Gibraltar (Columns of Hercules) and Pakistan (on the shores of the Indus). Runes have also appeared on small objects like pins, medals, and weapons.

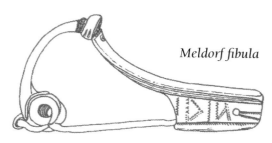

Meldorf fibula

The first written use of the runes was in the work of Tacitus, the famous Roman historian who, in 98 A.D., expressly cited the runes as a resource when discussing divination in his writings on Germany. Runes also appear in the so-called Runic poems that ancient troubadours from many cultures composed and recited and whose marvelous and fascinating adventures still captivate many readers today: the heroic deeds and stories of elves, men, and gods engaged in eternal battles against giants and dwarves. The oldest and most famous of these poems is the Edda, an Icelandic poem dating from 1000-1200.

THE RUNES AS A SYSTEM OF DIVINATION

At one point, the runes ceased functioning as alphabet and manifested themselves into a system of divination for obtaining advice and bringing clarity to a situation by analyzing its many points of view. This is precisely the point of this book: learning to consult the runes to resolve the predicaments and problems of everyday life.

Before examining each individual rune in detail, it is important to first be clear about a few points. My main point refers to divination itself: more than just being a tool for predicting the future, the runes can also serve as an instrument of self-knowledge, and they can help us to develop the psychic, spiritual, and psychological potential we already possess.

To understand what I mean, imagine a water-diviner looking for a source of water with his dowsing rod in an apparently arid zone. You are that water-diviner. The stick is the runes and the source of water represents the hidden resources that have only to be discovered and brought to light. The runes do not tell us exactly what will happen; rather, they work by outlining the situation and the energies it creates. It is up to you to use these energies in the way that best suit your needs.

Or imagine that we want to create a drawing: we can use many colored pencils or other supplies, but colors alone are not enough to create a beautiful picture. We also need artistic talent. This same way of thinking can be applied to the concept of Runic divination. The runes can suggest solutions to us, activate certain energies within us, and help us to realize our desires, but it is up to us to ensure that we take ownership of our own destinies.

Therefore, we cannot ask the runes to reveal future events in detail, but rather we need to ask them what would be the best course of action to take in order to manage a situation or event so that the outcome we wish for can be manifested. The best use of the runes is ultimately as a tool for self-improvement.

Not only can the runes be used as an oracle, but also have other functions that are extremely important. For example, they can be used for meditation. Focusing on one rune can enhance certain types of meditation. Specific runes can raise certain questions connected to its energy and significance. We can choose to concentrate on a specific question, meditating on all the various facets that arise and look to find more that one answer.

Another traditional use of the runes is magical. Runes have always been used as talismans to protect us in specific situations as well as enhancing some of our more positive characteristics. There are runes that have creative powers; runes capable of blocking negative energies; and runes perfect for consolation, reassurance, and manifesting certain situations or events. By becoming familiar with the various meanings of each individual rune, we can connect to them in an even more intimate manner.

CARING FOR YOUR RUNES

I believe the best way to learn to work with the runes is to incorporate them bit-by-bit into our daily lives. They are a useful tool for knowledge and can become a powerful ally that we care for and look after with love, just as we do with our homes or other treasured possessions.

How we store our runes is very important. You may choose to keep your runes in a velvet or silk bag in a color that you like or that signifies a certain meaning for you. Or, if you so choose, a wooden, stone, or ceramic bowl covered by a cloth works well, too. Whatever method you choose, store your runes in a place that's easily accessible at all times.

Whenever you feel the need to consult the runes, do so in quiet room. Take some time to relax and concentrate first. It takes time and patience in order to obtain good results, so if you are in a hurry, it is better to leave the consultation until later.

The surface on which we throw the runes is also important. It would be wise to cover this surface with a cloth that is used solely for this purpose. The cloth can be any color and fabric that you like. Burning a stick of incense will enhance concentration and gives the ritual a more formal feel.

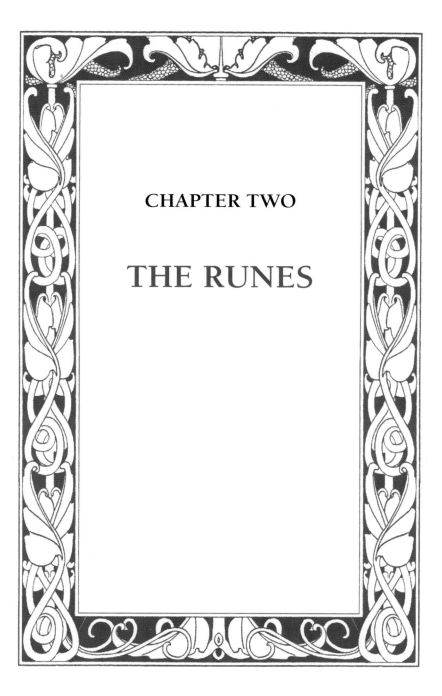

CHAPTER TWO

THE RUNES

Each rune is a synthesis of profound secrets that come from the Earth. To use the runes, one needs to know them; to know them requires discovering them slowly in all their meanings and aspects.

The runes have hundreds of facets, like a precious diamond, and can be used in many diverse situations and for many different reasons. Don't be in a hurry to discover everything about them immediately. Understanding the runes is something akin to the process of domesticating a small animal: time and patience are required, and your heart should guide you in your quest.

Personally, I suggest keeping a notebook handy where you can write down any observations and sensations that you may have as you study and use the runes. This notebook will become a valuable source of notes and observations, and enable you to easily evaluate your progress.

GETTING TO KNOW THE RUNES

In this chapter, we will get to the heart of the runes as we learn to work with each of them in detail. A specific page is dedicated to each rune and it is examined in each of its multiple aspects: for divination, for meditation, and its magical aspect.

The runes in the Futhark section are divided into three groups called Aett. Each Aett is made up of eight runes and takes its name from a Nordic god or goddess. For example, there is the Aett of Freyr, the Aett of Hagel, the Aett of Tyr, and the Aett of Odin (the twenty-fifth rune also known as the white rune).

FIRST AETT
Aett of Freyr, god of peace and fecundity:
- Fehu
- Uruz
- Thurisaz
- Ansuz
- Raidho
- Kenaz
- Gebo
- Wunjo

SECOND AETT
Aett of Hagel, god and guardian of the bridge of the rainbow:
- Hagalaz
- Nauthiz
- Isa
- Jera
- Eihwaz
- Perdho
- Algiz
- Suwilo

THIRD AETT
Aett of Tyr, god of war and justice:
- Tiwaz
- Berkana
- Ehwaz
- Mannaz
- Laguz
- Inguz
- Othala
- Dagaz

THE WHITE RUNE
- Odin

HOW TO READ EACH RUNE'S ENTRY

The separate entries for each rune are comprised of the following:

• **General information**: name variants, pronunciations of its name, and its ancient meaning.

• **Its essence**: an identity card of the rune that will highlight its most profound and elementary significance.

• **Key words**: a list of words connected to the emotional and existential areas where the rune acts. The key words express both the positive and negative qualities of the rune, which can then be used to the clarify context and questions during the interpretation process.

• **The message**: what the rune has to tell us about the situation in question and advice about how to better exploit the energies of the rune.

• **The warning**: the dark side of the rune. Our negative tendencies; the dangers we could possibly incur using the energies of the rune unknowingly.

• **The questions**: Each rune raises certain questions connected to its meaning. The possible questions are obviously more than what can be listed here in this book. If you keep a notebook with your observations, it can be useful to note all the questions that the various runes suggest during the session. This aspect is also useful during meditation sessions: choose a question that strikes you and meditate on it.

• **Talisman**: the magical aspects of the rune; the qualities that the rune potentiates and the areas of life that it protects and sustains.

1. FEHU

Pronunciation of the rune: F
Variations of the name: Feho in Old English; Feu in German; Fe in Viking
Ancient meaning: livestock

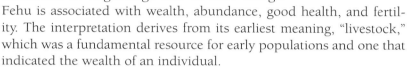

The Essence

Fehu is the first rune and for this reason, it is connected to beginnings and to new things. Fehu is associated with wealth, abundance, good health, and fertility. The interpretation derives from its earliest meaning, "livestock," which was a fundamental resource for early populations and one that indicated the wealth of an individual.

Key words

Positive: a new beginning, abundance, growth, trust, wellness, fertility, security, solidness, harmony.
Negative: the end of cycle, insecurity, inexperience, sterility, loss, arrogance.

The Message

Fehu indicates a good opportunity to realize your dreams. This rune is rooted in the material and sensual worlds and tells us that our earthly desires can be realized. It tells us the person we love shares our feelings; the efforts to obtain a certain result are repaid with acknowledgment and success crowns our endeavors. Life flows easily and we don't need to make too great an effort to find the resources we need. This is a good time to begin a new activity or to enjoy a well-deserved peace following a period of struggle and tensions.

The Warning

Fehu warns us of the risk of becoming too arrogant. Now that we have success at hand, we run the risk of behaving too euphorically, which could make us vulnerable and expose us to failure. More than ever, we need to be on guard. We need to be careful so that we don't behave in ways that will alienate others. It is important to have a

humble and dignified attitude and to share our wellbeing with those who are close to us.

The Questions
Are we content with our economic situation?
Do we feel a creative impulse within?
Do we want to become parents?
Are we at peace with ourselves?
Do we feel the need to seek medical advice?
Are we happy with our physical condition?
Are we content with our sex life?
Do we behave with generosity toward others?
Do we think we are superior to others?

Talisman
Fehu transits security and enterprise. It makes us strong and determined, full of intelligent ideas. It is a symbol of fertility and helps women who wish to become mothers, as well as artists who are looking for inspiration.

2. URUZ

Pronunciation of the rune: U
Variations of the name: Ur in Old English;
Uruz in German; Ur in Viking
Ancient meaning: bull

The Essence

Uruz literally means "Uro," the mythological, primordial bull associated with strength and primal energy found in Germanic cultures. Uruz is the male principle, representing virility and the vital breath that resides in each of us from the moment we are born. This rune is traditionally associated with audacity and with courage.

Key words

Positive: strength, tenacity, courage, resistance in adverse conditions, difficult tasks, good psycho-physical equilibrium, rapid actions, rewarding sexuality
Negative: aggressiveness, lust, anger, destruction, voraciousness, impulsiveness, weakness

The Message

Uruz urges us not to fear our instincts. There is a great potential in all of us, and it is our duty to direct this potential into constructive actions. People often encounter fear and resistance on the path to becoming themselves. The message from Uruz is to accept these challenges, to take on our own responsibilities, and to realize our destiny in the world. This is a time to work hard and to focus our energies towards our dreams. Only with courage and actions can we realize our potential.

The Warning

Uruz advises us to channel our energy in a positive way. Once we are conscious of our strength, we could be tempted to exploit it in an egotistical way. However, we should use it to overcome our limits and ourselves. Uruz is courage. Each time we experiment on ourselves,

every time we overcome a fear, we take a step towards self-realization. Furthermore, this rune warns of the danger of depending too much on others, as the base of every victory is autonomy.

The Questions
In what areas of our life do we exhibit courageous behavior?
When was the last time we were angry?
Are we responsible for ourselves?
How do we let off excess energy?
Do we feel dependent on others?
Do we act like adults, regardless of our age?
Are we frightened by our instincts?
Do we love our bodies?
What relationship do we have with respect to our aggressiveness and that of others?
Do our desires make us happy or depressed?

Talisman
Uruz transmits courage, vigor, and energy. It helps to unblock stagnant situations and gives us the necessary drive to deal with new ventures. It favors those who do physically demanding work and it removes sexual inhibitions.

3. THURISAZ

Pronunciation of the rune: TH
Variations of the name: Thornr in Old English;
Thurisaz in German; Thurs in Viking
Ancient meaning: thorn

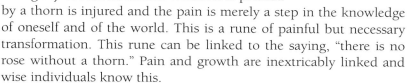

The Essence

Thurisaz means "thorn" and it is connected to the
ambiguity of consciousness. Whoever is pricked
by a thorn is injured and the pain is merely a step in the knowledge
of oneself and of the world. This is a rune of painful but necessary
transformation. This rune can be linked to the saying, "there is no
rose without a thorn." Pain and growth are inextricably linked and
wise individuals know this.

Key words

Positive: intuition, catharsis, purification, adventure, seduction,
choice, emotional intensity
Negative: ambiguity, shattering discovery, disturbances, self-injury,
unexpectedness

The Message

Thurisaz pushes us to go deeper. Only by having experiences in the
world can we understand it properly. Thurisaz speaks of the beauty
of thought, as sharp and shining as a blade. We need to learn to use
our intelligence as a sword to eradicate ignorance and illusions in the
world. This is a rune that encourages concentration and vigilance. It
often indicates a critical moment, but from this experience we can
learn a lot as long as we face it with determination and firmness.

The Warning

Thurisaz underlines a moment of doubt and uncertainty. We are torn
by two opposite tendencies: on the one hand, there is the seduction
of the future; and on the other, our attachment to the past. We need
to reflect before acting. Both impulsiveness and inertia will be damag-
ing. This is the moment to stop and think while trying to clarify all

aspects of the situation. It is better to act with caution than to have negative consequences in the future.

The Questions
Are we free spirits?
What disturbs us?
Are we fully living the present?
Are we afraid of discovering something that we would prefer not to know?
Are we in love with two people at the same time?
Are we tired of our routine?
Does the future worry us?
Have we hurt someone with our words?
Are we liars?
Do we live for our memories?

Talisman
Thurisaz guarantees great lucidity. It is useful in ambiguous situations and when we want to act with diplomacy. It is helpful for those facing tests.

4. ANSUZ

Pronunciation of the rune: A
Variations of the name: As in Old English;
Ansuz in German; As in Viking
Ancient meaning: mouth

The Essence

Ansuz is connected to words, language, and communication. Its ancient meaning is "mouth" and the essence of Ansuz is the teachings that have been passed down orally, leading to wisdom.

Key words

Positive: messages, fluid communication, comprehension, charismatic discourse, clarification of ideas, teachings, wisdom
Negative: falseness, opportunism, lies, biased advice, communication problems

The Message

Ansuz indicates novelty and openness towards the rest of the world. Communications flow freely and the trust we have in ourselves is a good base for ensuring that others appreciate us.
We are fascinating and hold great influence, which is necessary in order to constructively discuss projects with others. We manage to make ourselves understood and to carry our ideas forward without cowing to the opinions of others. This is a good time to plan for the future and to lay the foundation for projects that require a high level of thought.

The Warning

Ansuz warns us to avoid misunderstandings. Words are double-edged swords---sometimes truthful, sometimes false. In order to communicate effectively they must always be calibrated to the audience. At times, this rune can indicate gossip or conversations out of place--- excessive flippancy in talking can sometimes damage us, and it's best to keep harsh words to ourselves. Try to maintain a lucid

attitude both in discussing an idea and when listening to the opinions of others.

The Questions
Are we capable of acting on our ideas?
Do we maintain an independence of judgment?
Are we capable of keeping a secret?
Do we always speak the truth?
Are we fooled by appearances?
Are we victims of gossip?
Do we have enough trust in ourselves?
Are we capable of listening?
Do we express our feelings with ease?
Are we afraid of being tricked?

Talisman
Ansuz confers brilliance and clarity to ideas. It is very useful for creativity. It makes us empathetic and fascinating. It is useful for those who work closely with others.

5. RAIDHO

Pronunciation of the rune: R
Variations of the name: Raid in Old English;
Riado in German; Reid in Viking
Ancient meaning: chariot (of the sun)

The Essence
The Rune is related to the Sun and its journey across the sky. Raidho is a symbol both to phisical and metaphorical travel.
Its deeper meaning is that of progression, or evolution, toward a greater awareness.

Key words
Positive: travel, evolution, a shift, an important meeting, a realization, a result, an effective action
Negative: something unforeseen, a project obstructed, a battle for power, obscurity, reviewing and rethinking

The Message
Raidho directs us towards perfection. This rune indicates vitality and enthusiasm; fundamental qualities in undertaking any type of project. The sun shines in the sky and success will not be long in arriving. In this moment we can discover the qualities of leadership within ourselves. We have the capacity to work with others as well as to act autonomously. We are full of energy and the people we meet are struck by and fascinated with our charisma.

The Warning
The dangers that Raidho warns us about are those of imprudence and inflexibility. The negative message of this rune lies in the tendency to overextend our selves. Everything has its time. Raidho urges action, but also advises us to avoid impulsiveness. Furthermore, the fifth rune advises us to keep a proper distance between things and to not impulsively invade the territory of others. Raidho advises us that our energy must warm things, not burn them. There is a restlessness in

Raidho that must not be transformed into a tendency to dissipate one's talents and energies.

The Questions
Are we attracted to danger?
Do we wish to travel to faraway places?
What is our relationship to authority?
Are we capable of respecting a hierarchy?
What is our attitude towards others?
Do we trust our own judgment?
Do we feel energized?
Do we dream of a gypsy-like existence?
Are we capable of recognizing opportunities?
Do we act impulsively?

Talisman
Raidho provides great initiative and reinforces our ability to make decisions. It ensures protection during travels and increases charisma and leadership qualities.

6. KENAZ

Pronunciation of the rune: K or a hard C
Variations of the name: Cenk in Old English;
Kenaz in German; Kaun in Viking
Ancient meaning: torch

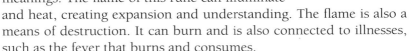

The Essence
Kenaz is connected to fire and all its multiple
meanings. The flame of this rune can illuminate
and heat, creating expansion and understanding. The flame is also a
means of destruction. It can burn and is also connected to illnesses,
such as the fever that burns and consumes.

Key words
Positive: inspiration, comprehension, compassion, heart and mind
united, passion, intensity.
Negative: illness, an agitated state, tension, destruction, a situation
spinning out of control

The Message
Kenaz indicates a moment of change: we feel full of passion and ardor
as something new enters our life in the form of an intense desire.
With Kenaz, we are ready to fall in love and to open our hearts, just
as we are ready to dedicate ourselves to enterprises that stimulate our
curiosity. This also is a good time to begin studying a new discipline.

The Warning
The sixth rune puts us on guard regarding explosive situations and
reminds us that we cannot always control everything. Passions burn
and can become uncontrollable. All we can do is acknowledge this
fact. Anger is part of human nature and we have been subjected to it
at times. We need not feel guilty for this, but remember that we can
try to succumb to it by developing compassion for our weaknesses
and those of others. Kenaz reminds us that we can learn from our
mistakes.

speaks of an unselfish love, which in its pureness generates other love.

The Questions
Are we open towards others?
What place does friendship have in our life?
Do we act in an unselfish way?
Are we able to recognize the worth of those close to us?
Do we wish ourselves well?
How well developed is our ability to be kind?
Are we able to care for others?
Do we wish to be diverted?
Do we take ourselves too severely?
Are we afraid of solitude?

Talisman
Gebo gives us the gift of acting in a balanced and diplomatic manner and protects those who have to enter into a contract. It gives kindness, a firmness of spirit, and an open heart.

8. WUNJO

Pronunciation of the rune: W or V
Variations of the name: Wyn in Old English
Ancient meaning: joy

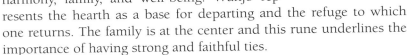

The Essence
The values that this rune brings with it are very ancient. The essences of Wunjo are joy, domestic harmony, family, and well-being. Wunjo represents the hearth as a base for departing and the refuge to which one returns. The family is at the center and this rune underlines the importance of having strong and faithful ties.

Key words
Positive: joy, heat, simplicity, abundance, sweetness, reciprocal help, solidarity, security, serenity, a sense of belonging
Negative: sadness, a sense of exclusion, solitude, arguments with people who are dear, a sense of being without roots

The Message
Wunjo speaks to the importance of our roots. Our family is the first tie that we have with the world and our love for them is the base of and the model for all our relationships. Wunjo represents a full life, lived with intensity and courage: being sure of ourselves and feeling connected to all that we have around us. We can enjoy day-to-day life because our soul is calm and serene and nothing really manages to bother us.

The Warning
Wunjo warns us not to block out negative experiences from the past. We need to find these experiences to move forward in the present. Our roots should be a point of departure, not a burden that stops us from evolving into the person that we really are. Another warning given by Wunjo is to not solicit affection but to find joy within our own beings. If we face the present with a calm soul, without doubts or suspicions, love will arrive spontaneously into our lives.

THE RUNES

The Questions

What type of relationship do we have with our family?

Do we feel nostalgic for the past?

Do we cherish our memories?

Do we experience the joy in our life?

How do we deal with our daily routines?

At times does it seem that we have never really grown up?

Do we feel that the time has come to start our own family?

Do we live the present intensely?

Do we get along with our friends?

What stops our desires?

Talisman

Wunjo helps us have harmonious relationships with our family and also protects couples. It stimulates understanding and harmony, ensures fidelity, and protects us from ambiguous situations.

9. HAGALAZ

Pronunciation of the rune: H
Variations of the name: Haegl in Old English;
Hagalaz in German; Hagal in Viking
Ancient meaning: hail

The Essence
Hagalaz signifies hail or sleet and alludes to the
cold winds of the north and bad weather. This
rune is apparently connected to destructive and dangerous forces
and indicates a period of crisis. However, Hagalaz also indicates an
exploding or explosive energy, one that we are forced to pay attention
to.

Key words
Positive: self-expression, a force that we can learn to control, concentration, explosions of happiness, untiring vitality
Negative: inner crisis, a shocking situation, a disaster, loss of a position and of power, argument, uncontrollable anger

The Message
The most important message Hagalaz conveys is to not be afraid
of our wild side. Often in our lives, we censor our aggression and
consider it totally negative, without realizing that this is an incorrect
attitude to have and not very courageous. Hagalaz underlines instead
the thought that our more tempestuous sides contain a great creative
potential---one we must embrace and manage.

The Warning
The ninth rune urges us to be more aware of our behavior. Anger
can be just as destructive if it is suffocated or negated as it is when
expressed in a violent or disruptive way. Hagalaz invites us to treat
our more primitive instincts like we would if we were the trainers of
ferocious animals. Only with knowledge and courage can we manage
to domesticate the beautiful tiger that roars within each of us and
ensure that it works for our good and for the good of all that surrounds us.

The Questions
When was the last time that we argued?
How do we express our anger?
Are we capable of facing situations that we don't like?
How do we react in the fact of arrogance?
Are we too hard on ourselves?
Do we act impulsively?
Are we afraid of our own reactions?
Do we know how to work in a group?
How do we vent our excess energy?

Talisman
Hagalaz strengthens our energy and makes us courageous and effective in our actions. It protects us against injustices and helps us to accept sudden changes.

10. NAUTHIZ

Pronunciation of the rune: N
Variations of the name: Nyd in Old English;
Naudiz in German; Nauo in Viking
Ancient meaning: necessity

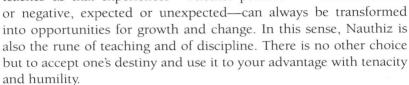

The Essence

Nauthiz has to do with need and necessity and
teaches us that experiences—whether positive
or negative, expected or unexpected—can always be transformed
into opportunities for growth and change. In this sense, Nauthiz is
also the rune of teaching and of discipline. There is no other choice
but to accept one's destiny and use it to your advantage with tenacity
and humility.

Key words

Positive: humility, wisdom, a serene attitude in the face of adversity,
resistance, teaching, altruism, renunciation
Negative: doubts, a difficult situation, a painful loss, the inability to
accept events, unsatisfied desires, unmotivated

The Message

Nauthiz instructs us to make necessity a virtue. A period of tests and
privations is not necessarily negative. This rune invites us to forge
discipline and inner strength. Everything has its season and for us,
this is the season for pruning away unnecessary things. Only in this
way will our potential flower again in its greatest capacity.
Nauthiz encourages us not to indulge and to use the utmost rigor and
severity with ourselves and with others; the results that we achieve
will astound everyone.

The Warning

The tenth rune puts us on guard with respect to an attitude that could
verge on fanaticism if taken to its extreme. Physical and spiritual privations can be useful trampolines to bounce toward the transformation
of certain situations, but what we absolutely must not do is to become
too inflexible and rigid. Another attitude that Nauthiz encourages

us to avoid is one of being disdainful, or from seeing ourselves as martyrs fighting alone against the world.

The Questions
What is our economic situation?
What are we willing to renounce?
Do we feel alone?
Are we ready to learn from new experiences?
Are we humble in our attitude with respect to what we don't know?
Are we reflective people?
Are we afraid of change?
Has the time come for us to study something new?
Are we capable of waiting?
Do we wish to be elsewhere?

Talisman
Nauthiz helps us overcome the most difficult situations with strength of spirit. It gives us a great willpower and spirit of sacrifice. It encourages the development of altruism and compassion towards others.

11. ISA

Pronunciation of the rune: I
Variations of the name: Is in Gothic; Isa in German; Iss in Viking
Ancient meaning: ice

The Essence

Isa means "ice" or "a piece of ice" and can be viewed as the embodiment of something cold, cutting, or delicate. The essence of this rune is ambivalent. On one hand, it is connected to concepts such as concealment and being inhospitable; on the other, it signifies extreme purity, beauty, and conservation. Like fire, ice and extreme cold are of great importance to man: they can kill as well preserve.

Key words

Positive: self-control, pure intent, clairvoyance, waiting patiently, far-sighted, strong willed, obstinacy, tenacity
Negative: being static, refusal to change, a long or painful waiting period, an unclear situation, superficial feelings, an inability to let things go

The Message

Isa teaches us to accept the status quo. This is not the time to act or give in to your impulses. What we must do is to try and perceive the situation and to understand it from all sides. Isa is the rune of lucid distancing from the group: only with a clear-sighted thought, like a piece of ice, will we be able to face up to events. We must put emotions aside and throw ourselves without fear into the high, cold spheres of abstract thought. We will return from our voyage lighter and wiser.

The Warning

Isa invites us to embrace a more open attitude and to accept the advice of others. The danger of this rune lies in an excessive rigidity that makes us myopic in the face of situations that we are currently experiencing. The key to winning is to break the static cycle and to

look at the present and the future with a fresh perspective or from a different point of view. Furthermore, Isa puts us on guard with respect to using words that are too sharp. We should avoid offending others and making enemies.

The Questions
Are we overly critical?
Are we prejudiced?
Do we hurt others without intending to do so?
What relationship do we have with cultures that are different from our own?
Are we sincere?
Are we afraid of being judged by others?
Do we have a sense of humor?
Are we experiencing a stagnant situation?
What changes could we make to our lives so that they better represent us?
What do we do to overcome our laziness?

Talisman
Isa protects us from gossip and from people who work against us. It gives us sharp reflexes and mental lucidity. It acts against negative thoughts.

12. JERA

Pronunciation of the rune: J or Y
Variations of the name: Ger in old English; Jera in German; Ar in Viking
Ancient meaning: year

The Essence
Jera is connected to the cycle of the seasons, especially to harvest time. This is a rune of happiness and abundance: the fruit is mature, the wheat is ready to be cut, and soil is at its peak of richness. Jera seems to suggest to us that after every winter, the summer arrives and that we must enjoy and celebrate each moment of our existence on the earth.

Key words
Positive: wellness, abundance, optimism, generosity, joy, brotherhood, a serene relationship, wishes realized, success attained after hard work
Negative: impatience, an arrogant attitude, a period of difficult work, overbearing, loss of energy, anxiety for the future

The Message
Jera invites us to enjoy the present. We have fought hard to get what we desired: now is the time to slow down and to admire the fruits of our labor. Often, the rush of everyday life doesn't allow us to fully enjoy the present and the affections of others. The message of Jera is to stop and to look around: in this moment we are surrounded by beauty. It would be a sin not to admire it and to let it capture us.

The Warning
Jera advises us to not let anxiety overtake us or be excessively greedy. The secret of happiness is in the here and now. It is from the present that we must depart in order to construct a better future. A sterile, frenetic manner will not get us to our destination any earlier. On the contrary, we risk losing sight of the importance and the beauty of daily life. We must force ourselves to take care of the details of our

life, to not neglect any area, and to have the maximum consideration for the affections of those who are dearest to us.

The Questions
Do we feel we are capable of realizing our dreams?
Are we afraid to be happy?
Do we reserve a place for the attentions of those we love?
Are we generous?
Are we capable of giving and receiving love?
How long ago was it when we last gave someone a gift?
Are we anxious about the future?
What sort of relationship do we have with money?
Are we happy with what we have?
Are we unrestrained in regard to eating and drinking?

Talisman
Jera puts us in the right state of mind to accept the seasons of life. It gives us optimism, good health, and encourages us to face changes and challenges head-on.

13. EIHWAZ

Pronunciation of the rune: IE
Variations of the name: Eoh in Old English; Ehwaz in German; Ihwar in Viking
Ancient meaning: tree

The Essence
Eihwaz means yew tree, a plant that in Germanic folklore is associated with death. As the tree is born from roots, so does the past gives birth to the future. This is what Eihwaz symbolizes. This rune is connected to inner strength and the capacity to find the necessary resources within ourselves.

Key words
Positive: inner strength, profound thoughts, indifferent feelings, actions carried out with honesty, removal from the daily routine
Negative: melancholy, the real or symbolic end to a situation, a painful transformation, an event endured, sadness, regret for the past

The Message
Eihwaz invites us to sink into the depths of situations and get to the root of them. We mustn't skim the surface; rather, we need to uncover that which is hidden. The thirteenth rune speaks to us of changes, mainly psychological, that we must deal with in order to evolve as individuals. It may not be a path of roses and flowers, but our job is to surge ahead without fear, venturing toward the unknown.

The Warning
Eihwaz warns us not to succumb to the pessimism that wants to overwhelm us. We all have a certain amount of darkness within ourselves. We should acknowledge it but it is not productive to fall prey to it. We have a great opportunity with this rune: elaborating a loss, to come to terms with the past, and to finally look at the future with renewed optimism and greater depth.

From a state of emotional confusion, something luminous and vital can be born. All that is required is a calm and aware attitude.

The Questions
How much does the past influence our present?
Do we feel melancholic?
Do we frequently daydream?
Do we have a habit of giving up?
Are we fatalistic?
Do we think that others don't understand us?
Is it difficult for us to express our feelings?
Do we have an unconfessed secret?
Do we take care of ourselves?
Do we think that some situations can never be changed?

Talisman
Eihwaz helps us overcome our deepest fears and gives us the courage to face difficult situations. It protects our sleep and encourages the study of philosophy and history.

14. PERDHO

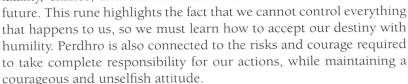

Pronunciation of the rune: P
Variations of the name: Peoro in Old English;
Perdhro in German; Pairtha in Viking
Ancient meaning: destiny

The Essence
Perdhro signifies destiny and is connected to
fatality, chance, and the inscrutableness of the
future. This rune highlights the fact that we cannot control everything
that happens to us, so we must learn how to accept our destiny with
humility. Perdhro is also connected to the risks and courage required
to take complete responsibility for our actions, while maintaining a
courageous and unselfish attitude.

Key words
Positive: a secret teaching, an unexpected event, a stroke of luck, a
letter, a surprise, a bold attitude, audacity
Negative: obstacles, ambivalence, good luck overturned, recklessness,
impulsiveness, ingenuity, excess

The Message
Perdhro celebrates the beauty of the unexpected. It indicates the
magic moment when many possibilities open up and there is neither
fear nor anxiety for the future. On the contrary, this instability is
experienced with a sense of electrifying euphoria. Routine may give
us a sense of security, but often clips our wings and our deepest and
true desires. The message that Perdhro brings is to let go and abandon
yourself to the beauty of the unknown. It will not be an easy path but
if we have enough courage, we can experience new and unexpected
situations.

The Warning
Mystery, the unknown, and the dark fascinate us, but this side of existence can end up becoming an obsession, making us lose our sense of
reality. Perdhro invites us to be prudent: a reckless and contemptuous
attitude in regard to danger will not get us far. On the contrary, it

will be the harbinger of false moves and errors of valuation. Perdhro invites us to look after ourselves and to try and protect our integrity in moments of confusion when nothing is as it seems.

The Questions
Do we desire an exciting life?
Are we capable of keeping a secret?
Are we attracted to ambiguous people?
Do we have a taciturn character?
When was the last time we told a lie?
Do we place ourselves in dangerous situations?
Are we capable of defending ourselves?
Do we fall in love with people who do not return our affections?
Are we interested in people who are very different from ourselves?

Talisman
Perdhro gives the gift of empathy and helps us to deeply understand the desires of others and as a consequence, to be great friends in life. It protects those with a secret.

15. ALGIZ

Pronunciation of the rune: Z
Variations of the name: Eohl in Old English;
Algiz in German; Ihwar in Viking
Ancient meaning: moose

The Essence

Algiz means "moose," a noble and untiring animal
that, for Germanic populations, indicates the ca-
pacity to defend oneself and persist in the face of adversity. Algiz is the
rune of strength and of protection, and of one who places him/herself
at the disposition of the community to ensure peace and well being.
The essence of this rune is generosity and the capacity to give without
expecting anything in return, just for the pleasure of helping a neighbor.

Key words

Positive: defense, protection, abundance, stability, an event, economic
solidity, victory over uncertainty
Negative: heavy obligations, impossibility to move, solitude, doubts,
indecisions, insecurity, inertia

The Message

Algiz speaks of the fundamental importance of willpower. In the
course of our lives, there will always be difficult situations. What
matters is the way in which we deal with them. The energy of Algiz
is one of generosity and selfless love: only by acting with a pure heart
can we overcome obstacles. Furthermore, Algiz encourages us not to
give up but to forge ahead with tenacity and perseverance. We may
lose some battles, but in the end we will win the war.

The Warning

Algiz inspires us to chase any shadow of egoism from our hearts and
minds. This is not the moment to act alone or for our own personal
advantage. The human spirit is often clouded by negative emotions,
such as jealousy, envy, or spite. The time has come to liberate ourselves from these negativities and to attain openness in respect to
others. Only in this way can we live our lives fully and intensely.

The Questions

Are we capable of accepting gifts from others?
How many true friends do we have?
Are we happy in the company of others?
Do we feel the need to stand out?
Do we desire what we haven't got?
Do we often feel jealous?
Do others confide in us?
How do we react in stressful situations?
Can we manage to put ourselves in someone else's shoes?
What would we like to change about ourselves?

Talisman

Algiz stimulates creativity and gives us the gift of resolving problems in an original and efficient way. It also gives us charisma and makes us popular and attractive.

16. SOWILO

Pronunciation of the rune: S
Variations of the name: Sigel in Old English;
Sowullo in German; Sol in Viking
Ancient meaning: wheel

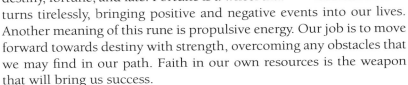

The Essence
Sowilo is closely connected to the concepts of
destiny, fortune, and fate. Fortune is a wheel that
turns tirelessly, bringing positive and negative events into our lives.
Another meaning of this rune is propulsive energy. Our job is to move
forward towards destiny with strength, overcoming any obstacles that
we may find in our path. Faith in our own resources is the weapon
that will bring us success.

Key words
Positive: victory, triumph, clear intentions, vitality, contagious happiness, a good disposition of the soul, health, creativity
Negative: stress, false destinations, excessive attachment to money, difficulty in living everyday life, pessimism

The Message
Sowilo invites us to measure our strengths and to use them only for
things that really interest us. The world is full of possibilities and it
is up to us to determine the road we must take. With a clear mind
and a pure heart, we must look within our souls to determine what
we truly desire. This rune brings good luck. Now that fortune smiles
upon us, it would be a shame not to seize the occasion, but we can
better exploit the situation only if we are truly self-aware.

The Warning
Sowilo advises us to not abuse our energies because they are not
limitless. It is unwise to cultivate unrestrained ambitions and poorly
disguised dreams of greatness. We must not bite off more than we
can chew because there is the danger of a great fall from grace if we
do. This is the time to reflect on the way we treat others. If we are too
arrogant or presumptuous, it is necessary to make amends.

The Questions
Is our happiness contagious?
How is our health?
Is our way of eating healthy?
Do we abuse our strengths?
Do we respect our bodies?
What wonderful dream are we about to realize?
Do we know when to keep silent?
Do we feel superior toward others?
What kind of relationship do we have with elderly people?
Do we know how to respect the hierarchy?

Talisman
Sowilo helps us clarify what we really want. It makes us vital, optimistic, and enhances our mood in a positive way. It protects us if we need to take a trip or during a sporting event.

17. TIWAZ

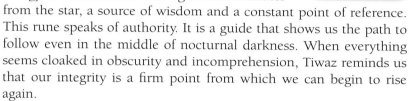

Pronunciation of the rune: T
Variations of the name: Tir in Old English; Tiewaz in German; Tyr in Viking
Ancient meaning: polar star

The Essence

Tiwaz means the "Polar Star." For this reason, its energy is connected to the light that emanates from the star, a source of wisdom and a constant point of reference. This rune speaks of authority. It is a guide that shows us the path to follow even in the middle of nocturnal darkness. When everything seems cloaked in obscurity and incomprehension, Tiwaz reminds us that our integrity is a firm point from which we can begin to rise again.

Key words

Positive: charisma, wisdom, authority, stoicism when facing the tests of life, lucidity, esteem gained thanks to one's actions.
Negative: coldness, emotional block, inability to understand the feelings of others, defeat, pretentious, errors in evaluation.

The Message

Tiwaz urges us to go straight along our path. When we have a clear objective in mind and know exactly what we want, it is easy for others who are less secure than us to feel jealous. Take no notice of them and continue in the direction you have chosen, making sure to pay attention to each and every detail. We are just a step away from success and cannot let anything distract us. In this moment, we must concentrate all our energies on a single objective.

The Warning

Tiwaz tells us to overcome the arrogance that can arise from experiencing a moment of success. Our job is to progress, not to rest on our laurels and judge others from a superior position.
Try to collaborate with those who surround us and to resist displaying any excessively authoritarian behavior that could turn against us in

the future. Enjoy success; live it with rightful satisfaction but not with an excessive or misleading euphoria.

The Questions
What sector of your life gives you the most satisfaction?
Are we ever brusque with others?
Are we able to share success with those close to us?
Do we respect the feelings of others?
Do we feel overly ambitious?
What are we capable of doing in order to attain success?
What parts of our lives are we neglecting?
Are we receptive to flattery?
Do others listen to us?
Are we natural leaders?

Talisman
Tiwaz sharpens intelligence and helps us to reach success and to overcome obstacles. It gives the gift of a great ability to resist and protects us from gossip and the envy of others.

18. BERKANA

Pronunciation of the rune: B
Variations of the name: Beorc in Old English;
Berkana in German; Bjarkan in Viking
Ancient meaning: swan

The Essence

Berkana means "swan" and is connected to beauty and femininity. The rune symbolizes a woman in all her traditional roles: mother, wife, sister, and daughter. This rune has a receptive energy, and its strength lies in welcoming, understanding, and nurturing. Berkana has a great creative force. It is the rune of sensuality and maternity and is closely connected to the arts in the sense of energy that creates and transforms.

Key words

Positive: creation, sensitivity, artistic talent, aesthetic sense, love of children and animals, maternity, the ability to nurture
Negative: possessiveness, problems in the family, creative block, sterility, up-rooted, difficulty in finding one's path, lack of tenderness

The Message

Berkana speaks of tenderness as a necessary energy for taking action in the world. Regardless of our sexual identity, we are living in profound harmony with our feminine side in this moment. We feel compassionate and full of inspiration. There is nothing competitive in our interactions with others. We are motivated by the desire to understand them and make them feel good. Our creative abilities are highly stimulated by this rune. This is an excellent opportunity to create something. Berkana also speaks to the desire to be parents and to start a family.

The Warning

Berkana pressures us to get in touch with the most vulnerable parts of ourselves. We must take care of these parts and become parents to ourselves first. This is the time to heal the wounds of childhood. Only by recognizing our own weaknesses can we become a strong adult.

We must not make the mistake of only looking after certain aspects of our beings, neglecting those parts that are more fragile.

The Questions
Are we capable of caring for others?
Do we desire to bring something into the world?
What emotions do children inspire in us?
What sort of relationship do we have with our parents?
Are we creative?
Do we have trouble expressing our emotions?
Are we sometimes ashamed by what we feel?
Do we frequently blush?
Are we at ease in the midst of people?
Would we like to have a pet to look after?

Talisman
Berkana protects children and women and stimulates our creativity. It assists in actual and symbolic births. It provides serenity and makes us generous and altruistic.

19. EHWAZ

Pronunciation of the rune: E
Variations of the name: Eh in Old English;
Ehwaz in Gothic; Ior in Viking
Ancient meaning: horse

The Essence
Ehwaz literally means "horse". This rune is closely connected to a trip, both in the physical and in the metaphorical or spiritual sense. It is the rune of progress—of advancement in a career—and it indicates the importance of finding one's place in the world.

This rune is connected to independence and the effort required in obtaining it. Its energy helps one to come out of one's shell and to open up to the world.

Key words
Positive: alliance, trip, discovery of faraway worlds, expression of one's potential, fame, great energy, resources
Negative: impatience, overstepping one's boundaries, fear of expressing oneself, shyness, laziness, forced inactivity

The Message
Ehwaz calls us to action and movement. Everything transforms and our job is to follow the flow of events without becoming static and fearful. Life is an adventurous trip! This is the message of this rune that has a huge potential of energy and success within it. Whatever age we are, it is never too late to begin a new undertaking, to try something different, or to enhance a capacity that has remained latent or unexpressed.

The Warning
Ehwaz pushes us to break the sterile, continual circle that surrounds us. If this is what we feel, then Ehwaz advises us to stop and reflect. The dark sides of this rune are impatience and the desire for something, regardless of the cost, even if we do not have the means to obtain it. If a situation works out well, it does so because it was well organized. Slow the pace and take care of all the details before acting.

The Questions
Where would we like to be at this moment?
Do we often daydream?
Do we worry about the small things?
Are we attracted to exotic and distant places?
Do we desire that which is not ours?
Do we work well in the company of others?
Do we find strength in numbers?
Do we make friends easily?
Do we want to learn a foreign language?
Do we usually manage to realize our dreams?

Talisman
Ehwaz protects travel and gives great speed to the actions of everyday life. It makes unions solid and encourages a serene married life.

20. MANNAZ

Pronunciation of the rune: M
Variations of the name: Man in Old English;
Mannaz in Gothic; Madr in Viking
Ancient meaning: humanity/mankind

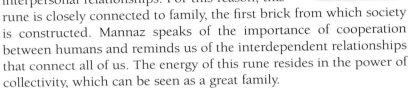

The Essence

Mannaz means "humanity" in the context of interpersonal relationships. For this reason, this rune is closely connected to family, the first brick from which society is constructed. Mannaz speaks of the importance of cooperation between humans and reminds us of the interdependent relationships that connect all of us. The energy of this rune resides in the power of collectivity, which can be seen as a great family.

Key words

Positive: honest social relationships, the ability to cooperate, collective dreams, help received and given, harmonious family life, friendship
Negative: the inability to connect with others, solitude, egoism, little practical sense, not in harmony with one's emotions, insensitive.

The Message

Mannaz enhances the idea of a universal mind that encompasses all of us. Even in the most extreme situations it is good to remember that we are never alone, but that we are part of the great human family. The rune places emphasis on the sentimental and on blood ties and on their extreme importance. Communication and exchange are two very important concepts. Union makes for strength. Friendship and actions that combine complementary energies will attain great results.

The Warning

Mannaz warns us to not close ourselves off too much. As much as we can be strong and autonomous, it is important to have external points of reference. The clan—in this case, your family and group of friends—is the scaffolding of our lives: it helps and sustains us. If we have had some disagreements lately with somebody close to us, the time has come to smooth things out.

The Questions

Are we capable of expressing our affections?
Do we feel gratitude towards others?
When was the last time we confided in someone?
Do we really feel close to our friends?
Are we able to get involved in collective projects?
Do we actively participate in family life?
Do we feel alone and misunderstood?
When was the last time we invited someone to our home?
Do we worry about the wellbeing of others?
Do we feel the need to be hugged?

Talisman

Mannaz protects us in legal matters and when interacting with others.
It stimulates comprehension and group work. It increases loyalty and
honesty.

21. LAGUZ

Pronunciation of the rune: L
Variations of the name: Lagu in Old English;
Laguz in German; Log in Viking
Ancient meaning: water

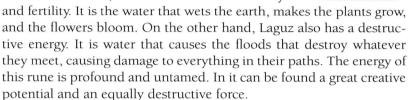

The Essence
Laguz means "water" and has a double essence.
On the one hand, it is connected to creativity
and fertility. It is the water that wets the earth, makes the plants grow,
and the flowers bloom. On the other hand, Laguz also has a destructive energy. It is water that causes the floods that destroy whatever
they meet, causing damage to everything in their paths. The energy of
this rune is profound and untamed. In it can be found a great creative
potential and an equally destructive force.

Key words
Positive: fantasy, fertility, inner evolution, inspiration, potency of one's
wishes, romanticism, being in love, desire for beauty
Negative: daydreaming, illusions, bursts of anger, sexual inhibitions,
scarce self-knowledge

The Message
Laguz suggests listening to our deepest id, to our dreams, and to our
instincts. It is the rune of the subconscious and of premonitions: its
energy is oriented toward the perceptions of the emotive currents
that circle around us. This rune gives preference to creative intelligence over a cold analysis of reality. The key to resolving eventual
problems that present themselves resides more in intuition than in a
more cerebral approach.

The Warning
Laguz nudges us to take the reins of our life in hand. Perhaps we feel
like a raft adrift in a stormy sea: we are drowning. For this reason, the
moment has come to dip into our deepest hidden strengths. It is a
critical time but nothing is lost because, like water, our spirit knows
to regenerate itself in order to gush clearer and purer than before.

The Questions
Are we in contact with our subconscious?
Are we aware of our creative energy?
Do we feel more alive when we are in love?
Are we afraid of our reactions?
Do we repress anger?
What relationship do we have with women? With men?
Do we like cooking for others?
Do we repress our worries?
What is our weak point?
Are we in need of healing?

Talisman
Laguz enhances therapeutic gifts and makes us more empathetic and compassionate. It protects sleep and helps us to interpret dreams. It provides flexibility and resistance in emotionally complicated situations.

22. INGUZ

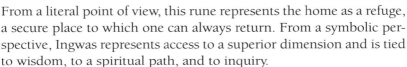

Pronunciation of the rune: NG
Variations of the name: Ing in Old English;
Ingwaz in German; Iggwis in Gothic
Ancient meaning: entrance

The Essence

Ingwas means "entrance." The essence of this
rune can be read on several different levels.
From a literal point of view, this rune represents the home as a refuge,
a secure place to which one can always return. From a symbolic perspective, Ingwas represents access to a superior dimension and is tied
to wisdom, to a spiritual path, and to inquiry.

Key words

Positive: faithfulness, spirituality, deep thoughts, inner growth,
meditation, tranquility, domestic joy, the hearth
Negative: restlessness, spiritual crisis, doubts about one's abilities,
sacrifices, unrequited love, a sudden banishment from the family

The Message

Ingwas underlines the importance of serenity and harmony within
the family. At this time, it is not good for us to be alone. In order to
undertake a path towards a higher spirituality, we need the tranquility
that comes from the affection of our loved ones. Ingwas speaks to
order and cleanliness. Our mind is like a house: in order for it to
function properly, it must be kept in order.

The Warning

Ingwas encourages us to take reach out to others. There are moments
when we feel alone and misunderstood. In more extreme cases, we
see others as enemies and we close ourselves off even more. This
attitude feeds on itself, generating feelings of anger and frustration
within us. The only way for us to break this cycle is to have a bit of
faith in others and open ourselves up to them. The fear of being rejected blocks us. If we overcome this fear, we can enter into a superior
dimension that is dominated by peace and cooperation.

The Questions
What do we actually do for others?
Do we hold rancor towards someone?
Do we keep our house in order?
How are we viewed in our workplace?
Are we at peace with ourselves?
Is our family life a source of joy?
Do we feel emotionally and physically fit?
Do we take care of our personal hygiene?
Do we recognize the good qualities in our partner?
Are we ready to help others?

Talisman
Ingwas protects the house, the family, and children. It guarantees understanding and friendship, makes us happy, strong, generous, and ready to improve ourselves.

23. OTHALA

Pronunciation of the rune: O
Variations of the name: Ethel in Old English;
Othal in German; Othala in Gothic
Ancient meaning: nobility

The Essence
Othala literally signifies nobility and refers to
all the things that we have inherited from our
ancestors. Our roots are very important and we must recognize them
in order to evolve as humans. Othala reminds us that we are the fruit
of a long history and that there were those who worked hard in order
for us to be who we are today.

Key words
Positive: prosperity, heredity, the importance of the past, abundance,
building strong ties, attachment to one's country, respect for traditions
Negative: little substance, economic problems, frauds, prejudices, difficulty in finding one's path, excessive parental influence, pessimism

The Message
Othala exhorts us to value our feelings and to build strong ties. Its
energy is directed toward the affective nucleus of life, which is faced
with a global vision that embraces the past, present, and future. This
rune highlights blood ties. As much as these relationships are stormy
or have been so in the past, they nevertheless remain important. To
remove one's self totally is only an illusion. It is important to gather
what is good and to smooth out misunderstandings as they happen.

The Warning
Othala puts us on guard with respect to individualistic and rebellious
behaviors. For each one of us it is important to emancipate ourselves
and to find our own path, but to do so we really need to look at our
past in a calm manner and with gratitude. If this does not happen, our
attempts at independence will be childlike and will not have the seriousness required to make them effective and adult. Leave old and infantile
behavior behind and accept the challenge of growth with courage.

The Questions
Are we overly attached to our childhood?
Do we always behave in the same way?
Are we egotistical?
Are we afraid of new things?
Do we live with regrets?
Do we have respect for traditions?
What do we struggle to abandon?
Does fear block our emotions?
Are we often defensive?
Do we respect hierarchy?

Talisman
Othala consolidates unions and creates favorable conditions for increasing one's patrimony. It represents wellbeing, prosperity, and protects financial enterprises.

24. DAGAZ

Pronunciation of the rune: D
Variations of the name: Daeg in Old English;
Dagaz in German; Dags in Gothic
Ancient meaning: the light of midday

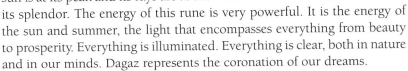

The Essence

Dagaz is connected to the light of midday, when the
sun is at its peak and its rays are at the maximum of
its splendor. The energy of this rune is very powerful. It is the energy of
the sun and summer, the light that encompasses everything from beauty
to prosperity. Everything is illuminated. Everything is clear, both in nature
and in our minds. Dagaz represents the coronation of our dreams.

Key words

Positive: success, understanding, popularity, artistic gifts, amiability,
happiness, good news, birth, requited love
Negative: mistrust, loss of hope, anxiety for the future, a failed project, the end of a cycle, broken connection, disillusionment

The Message

The trip has been long and difficult but we have finally arrived at
our destination. Dagaz speaks to success and the realization of our
dreams. With this rune, we have achieved a rare moment of equilibrium and we are at the peak of our splendor. We manage to express
ourselves with ease and fluidity and others are fascinated and attracted
to our charisma. There is nothing unharmonious or aggressive in our
behavior. On the contrary, we are aware of our value. For this reason
we have no need to give expression to it through arrogance.

The Warning

Dagaz places emphasis on self-esteem. Many of our problems and
failures derive from uncertain attitudes we hold and the scarce esteem
we have in ourselves. How can we convince others of our worth if we
are the first to have many doubts? Dagaz encourages us to be clear in
our hearts and to love ourselves. A sympathetic attitude towards ourselves will be the driving force behind any future victory.

The Questions
Do we feel beautiful?
Are we attracted to success?
Do we bring happiness to our group of friends?
What do we feel when we see a child?
Do we like to decorate our home?
Do we love surprises?
Do we feel at ease in the company of others?
What new challenges await us?
Do we feel capable of attracting a mate?
Are we clear about our objectives?

Talisman
Dagaz helps us understand what we want and to develop self-esteem and security. It makes us courageous and capable of participating. It protects the couple and improves sexual relations.

25. ODIN
THE WHITE RUNE

Odin is a special rune. For this reason, I have not provided an interpretation guide as I did for the previous runes. It possesses an energy that must be interpreted in relation to the other runes. Odin is not part of the runic alphabet, does not have a sound, and is not represented by any sign. It symbolizes silence, the blank page that has yet to be written, and the tabula rasa. In a single word, Odin represents fate.

Odin is imponderable. It symbolizes the chaos in which all possibilities are available and where everything can dissolve. It is the rune of the unknown and of the unconscious and has roots in that part of ourselves where we are afraid to knowingly venture. Its energy is strong and primordial and is closely connected to primary needs, to instinct, and the proverbial phases when our desires are not yet organized in stable and organic thoughts.

Odin is the rune of a thousand possibilities and for this reason its dark side is represented by indecision, the incapacity to choose, and excessive pulsations of self-destruction that lie dormant in all of us. We must be careful not to use our unconscious energies in a way that is potentially destructive. On the contrary, if directed in a harmonious way, they can be trampolines that take us in the direction of profound transformation.

Odin highlights the innate limits of humans and the fact that it is impossible for us to control everything. As much as we try to react to reality and to improve ourselves, there is always an element that escapes our control. All that we can do is to accept that fact and boldly dismantle all the superficial trappings that do not allow us to move forward.

When Odin appears near another rune, it overturns the meaning of that rune. Odin is the rune that destroys every certainty and can be compared to destructive phenomena: earthquakes, floods, and storms.

It is up to us to gather and use the strength of Odin in the best way possible. This is not an easy undertaking as it requires courage and a certain level of personal understanding. Odin and the other runes ask us, each in its own specific way and particular context, to evolve and participate in order to truly become who we are.

After all, apart from our chains, what do we have to lose?

CHAPTER THREE

USING
THE RUNES

The runes are valued for their mysterious power. From the moment they are called into action, they are an important instrument of knowledge. Just as a pearl necklace or a precious gem acquires life and beauty when it is worn, so do the runes become energized and give wisdom each time they are used.

We are at the beginning of a fascinating journey; one rich with surprises that has the potential to guide and enrich us for the rest of our lives. As with all journeys, it begins with a single step, building until we have reached our destination. Once we become familiar with the runes and with their significance and meanings, it is possible to begin to utilize them. As you have seen in the previous section, the runes can be used in many different ways. In this part of the book, we'll examine the runes in detail and look at the way they are most typically used: divination, meditation, and ritual. Here are some general instructions regarding the use of this precious instrument.

RUNES: WHERE, WHEN, FOR WHOM

I never tire of repeating that the runes will become an intimate part of your daily routine as you slowly learn to use them. This does not mean that you have to use them in that way.

If you do use them often, make sure that your interactions with the runes do not become stale or boring in any way. A certain ritual must be followed and it is essential that a certain amount of respect be used when interacting with the runes.

Where

I personally do not go anywhere without bringing one of my bags of runes with me. However, I would not think of using them in a crowded café, even if I felt I had a need to do so in that moment.

When using the runes, it is important to find a quiet and protected place where one feels safe and at ease. A room in your house can be dedicated specifically to using the runes. You'll want to purify the space by burning some incense sticks. Or if you want to interact with the runes outdoors, you can choose a place that inspires you in some way. As I am a great lover of nature, I have often read the runes under the branches of a tree in the middle of a park.

Another piece of advice when using the runes is to have a specific piece of cloth on which to place the runes when observing and interpreting them. There are many beautiful pieces of cloth in satin or velvet available for sale, but you may use any type of fabric you wish.

When

Knowing when to use the runes is a delicate and subjective question. It is something that varies from person to person because the relationship we have with the runes is very intimate, personal, and evolves over time. A general rule is wait to feel "inspired" but don't be afraid to ask questions that may seem silly or superficial. At times it may be curiosity that calls you to the runes, but even this is a valid reason to use them. Generally, if you feel the need to consult the runes, that is reason enough to use them. It may not seem like profound reason at that moment, but as you work with the runes, you may find yourself exploring some very important questions and answers.

The most important lesson here is to treat the runes with respect and seriousness and do not use them as a pastime or a simple game. By doing this, you would limit the use of this powerful tool.

For Whom

When people learn that you know how to read the runes, they may ask you for a reading. How do you control this?

The runes are an important means for understanding oneself and improving the environment around us. There is no reason to refuse to help others, but do so only if you think reading for others is absolutely necessary. Never feel obliged to do so. If you do it out of obligation, the runes will not function properly and you will not do yourself or others any favors. In this situation, you could say, "Right now I don't feel that I can read the runes for someone else. If it's important to you, I'll show you how to do it and we can interpret them together."

If you do read the runes for others, I suggest keeping a bag of runes that can be used specifically for conducting readings for others. When they ask you to read the runes, use those specific runes for the reading. You could also let the person involved throw and read the runes, and you can guide them and provide advice. In every situation, it's best to follow your instinct and your own feelings.

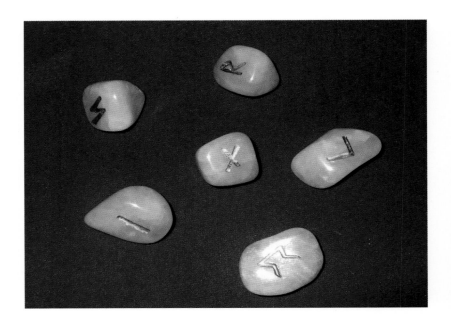

THE RUNES AS DIVINATION TOOLS

In his fundamental work on the Germanic population, Tacitus gave us information about using runes as a divinatory oracle. To use the runes in this way, you can utilize the many types of oracular spreads that already exist. Once you feel secure in your abilities to read and interpret the runes, you can invent your own spreads. To begin, let's look at the more well-known and utilized spreads.

Oracle of the three stars

To begin our journey with the runes, we can use this very simple example of a layout, through which we can bring light to a situation by following its evolution in time: the past, present, and future. Choose three runes and place them in a horizontal line. Reading from left to right, the first rune represents the past and root of the situation, the second is the present, and the third is the development of the situation in the future.

Example

I met a boy I liked and we saw each other a few times but now it seems he has lost interest. I want to know something more about the situation. The runes picked are Tiwaz (the past), Berkana (the present), and Nauthiz (the future).

• Tiwaz: In the past this boy was always very independent, proud of his successes, and never really embraced his more sensitive and kind side. He was more interested in dominating others and being free without having ties to others.

• Berkana: Now, because of meeting me (or the person asking the question if you are reading the runes for another person), his outlook has changed. For the first time he is experiencing the beauty that comes from connecting with others, being cared for, and feelings of understanding and empathy. Unfortunately this has created conflict with the core of his wild and autonomous personality.

• Nauthiz: The future seems to be in my hands. Great patience will be necessary to erode the fears of this person that interests me. Nevertheless, with a strong-willed patience, there is a good chance of overcoming these emotional obstacles.

The Oracle of the Twelve Houses

This layout is easy to use but it is also very precise and articulated. It helps give the person asking the question a complete view of the situation. As it involves a minimum of twelve runes, it is a good way to begin familiarizing oneself with the meanings of the runes. Here is how to proceed.

Phase One

Randomly pick twelve runes from the bag and place them in a circle. You'll want to start the reading at the top, moving in a clockwise direction. Each rune corresponds to an astrological house and shines light on the situation in question through its significance on the area connected to the corresponding house. Consequently, you need to interpret each rune by associating it with the meaning of the house in which it is found.

Here are the meanings relevant to the twelve houses:
I: your personality and psychophysical condition
II: your attitude regarding money and material goods
III: all types of communication, contact with the environment, attitude towards studying, exams, small journeys
IV: your family, your relationship with your heritage and traditions from one's country of origin, the home
V: love, children, creativity, games and fun, free time
VI: routine, work and obligations, caring for animals, health, diet
VII: relationships of any kind, business matters, interactions with others
VIII: sexuality, relationship with death and ancestors, inheritance (material and moral)
IX: that which is far away, journeys, spirituality
X: emancipation, autonomous work, social goals, successes
XI: friendship, groups, social life, collaboration with others, associations of all kinds
XII: tests, solitude, hidden talents, inspirations

In each of these existential sectors, the runes selected provide a general overview of that aspect of your life in the present moment. If you wish to have an indepth reading and see how various situations will evolve in the future, it is possible to do a second extraction.

Phase Two (optional)
Complete the interpretation of the first twelve runes and then place another twelve in correspondence to the first group (only one rune will remain unused), forming another circle. This time, contrary to the first extraction, proceed in a counterclockwise direction starting from the 11 o'clock position on a normal clock face, where the rune relative to the XII house is positioned. Now you can interpret the oracle in detail, remembering that the new runes represent the future that waits for you in each area.

Example

For the I house, the runes Laguz and Algiz are successively selected. Interpreting Laguz, you realize that your personality is that of a dreamer and independent. You love travel, both in a physical and metaphorical sense, and you are good at looking at a problem from all sides. However, you suffer because you are often indecisive and hesitant about everything. Algis introduces an element of being strong-willed into your character, which is just what it is missing. The rune encourages you to throw yourself into the fray and invites you to think about this question "What defect of mine would I like to change?"

Classical Oracle

This interpretation system uses all the runes and is similar to the system that was used in ancient times. Due to its complexity, it is better to begin using this method when you have become sufficiently proficient in understanding the runes and in interpreting their meanings.

Take the bag of runes, shake it, and tip it out onto a small cloth. Place a small pendant or other object (it is best if the object is connected, even in a symbolic way, to the question you are about to ask) in the center of the cloth. For example, you can use a candle, heart-shaped bowl, or ring for a question about love. Once the runes have been thrown, the first thing to you should do is look at them together and begin to evaluate their positions.

Next, divide the cloth into four quarters, with the pendant or object in the center. If there are more runes in the upper part of the cloth, the situation is generally positive or will be improving. But if most of the runes are in the lower sections of the cloth, things are going in the opposite direction.

The same goes for the right and left side of the cloth. If there are more runes on the left side, the situation you are thinking about has a prevalent emotional component, more inner thought than practical thought. If there are more runes on the right side, the problem is more of a concrete and objective kind.

Another element to pay attention to is how the runes are placed on the cloth. Some will be near others, forming a kind of group, while others will be isolated. In interpreting them, the groups of runes should be done first as they represent the primary aspects of the problem. The isolated runes should be examined later as they represent the secondary aspects of the problem.

Once an overview of the runes has been taken, the first thing to be done is interpret the runes that appear face up (with the symbol visible) and ignore the runes that are face down (with the symbol hidden from view). The runes that appear in the same group should be interpreted together.

The significance of a rune (positive or negative, emotional-affective or concrete-objective) depends on its position on the cloth. Those nearest the center are the most important and give what can be called the general imprint of the answer. Those furthest away represent the secondary aspects or hidden sides of the problem. Those in the upper quadrants are more positive whereas those in the lower quarters are more negative. For example, you could use the message of the rune to interpret the upper part and the warnings of the rune for the bottom part.

Initially this method can seem to be a bit difficult, but it is extremely effective, flexible, and fascinating, as well as being an excellent mental exercise. As you gain experience with reading the runes, you will appreciate this spread all the more.

An expert reader of runes should also take into account these factors:
• Runes near each other belong to the same Aett (discussed in the second chapter of this book) and have a major influence over the interpretation.
• A line of runes that goes from the center toward the outside indicates the evolution of the situation.
• Groups of runes that appear face down (their signs not visible) represent unexpressed potential or blocked energy.
• The position of the rune Odin indicates the crux of the situation (be careful to recognize it amongst all the runes that are face down).

As you can see, the Classical Oracle provides a very complex, accurate, and profound interpretation. Do not be discouraged if it is difficult the first time you use this method. It will become an extraordinary means of divination with just a bit of practice.

Example

I have a job interview in a few days and I am very agitated. I would like to have an objective view of the situation. I begin by placing the pen that I usually use for signing contracts in the center of the cloth. I throw the runes and begin to count. In the upper part of the cloth, there are ten runes. In the lower quadrant there are eleven, which is a sign that the situation leans toward the negative. There are twenty runes to the left of the pen and five on the right. This means that the conflicts and negative factors are internal and not influenced by the surrounding environment.

I now concentrate on the right side of the cloth where the five runes have fallen in a group. This family of runes is very important because it sheds light on what will be the concrete issues or strong points for the interview. I then move to the left side of the cloth. Here is a small family of three runes, which concentrate on my insecurities and will advise me on how to resolve them.

Next, I'll move on to interpreting the isolated runes. There is one positioned right next to the pen. I pay particular attention to this rune because this is the rune whose energy I must "use" to sign the contract. This rune is Kenaz, and its key phrase is "heart and mind united."

Even without considering every interpretation possible for this particular rune, the runes provide a very accurate and profound read on the situation. When using the oracle for the first time, limit yourself to concentrating on certain aspects of the interpretation, as in the example above. When you have acquired more experience using the runes, you can call on a greater number of interpretations for an even more profound and detailed reading.

Advice for the week
The following layout is extremely simple and is useful for attaining advice on what course of action to take for the day. It's also ideal for determining the day's dominant energy.

On Sunday evening, take out seven runes (one for each day of the week) and place them in a line on the cloth without looking at them. Cover them with a corner of the same cloth. Each morning, as soon as you wake up, uncover the rune that corresponds to that day (the first is Monday, the second, Tuesday, etc.). Try to extract a word or phrase that will guide you during the day. Later on you can think about the ways the rune has influenced your day.

Please note that if you use this system for throwing the runes, it is very useful to have a notebook or a diary to write down which runes you have extracted. This will help you to reflect and meditate on past events in relation to the rune that you have just selected. As a result, the notebook becomes an extraordinary tool for developing your relationship with the runes and for improving your interpretation skills.

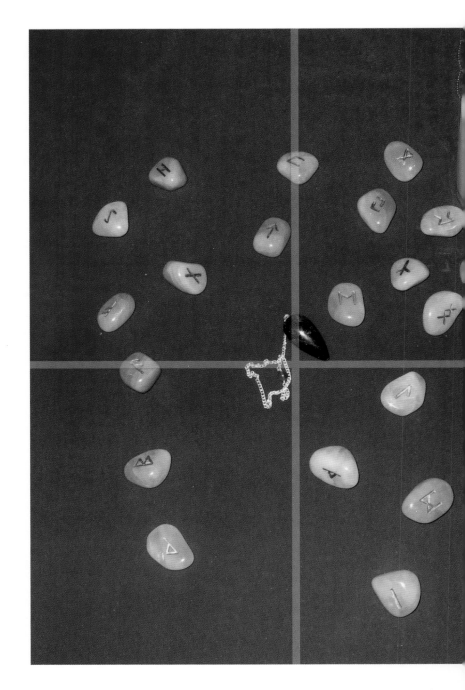

left: mentally divide the table into four quadrants.
- upper right: positive and practical
- lower right: negative and practical
- lower left: negative and emotional
- upper left: positive and emotional

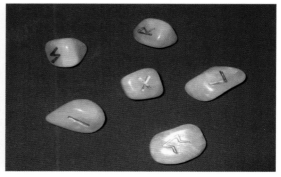

above: runes appearing in a circle or in a group indicate a stable situation

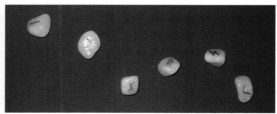

above: runes appearing in a line indicate a dynamic situation

ADVICE FOR INTERPRETATION

A concentration of runes in the upper quadrant: a situation that is generally positive.

A concentration of runes in the lower quadrant: a situation that is generally negative.

A concentration of runes on the left side: a situation with a strong emotional and personal influence.

A concentration of runes on the right side: a situation with a strong practical and objective influence.

The runes mostly appear in a group with a few isolated runes to the side: a clear and well-organized situation of great importance.

The runes fall into different groups with a few runes isolated to the side: a complex situation with different points of view or choices, which have yet to be made.

The runes fall into different groups with many runes isolated to the side: a confused or contradictory situation that could evolve in many different ways.

Most of the runes are face-up (with the symbol visible): a stable situation, constant over time.

Most of the runes are facedown (with the symbol not visible): a fluctuating situation, a long way from expressing its full potential.

A group of runes in a circle or in a group: a stable influence; a static situation.

A group of runes in a line (straight or irregular): a changing influence; a dynamic situation.

A group of runes belonging to the same Aett: meaning reinforced.

Let me provide you with an example. On Monday, the rune I extract is Gebo. The advice for that rune is: "Have faith in the world." The energy of the rune will influence my exchanges, dialogues, and communications with others throughout the day.

USING THE RUNES FOR MEDITATION

There are many ways of meditating with the runes. The more traditional way is a way in which one concentrates and gradually gains an understanding of the meanings, symbols, and materials relative to the runes. Other ways include focusing on a problem or question and using the energies of the runes to resolve the problem or question. I'll focus on three types of meditation in particular.

Classical Meditation

Meditation can last a few minutes or many hours. I personally would suggest that if you wish to use the runes for this purpose, meditate for at least five minutes every morning. Little by little, as you gain confidence in this practice, you can increase the time that you dedicate to meditation. While I think that twenty minutes is an ideal amount of time to spend on meditation, your situation will depend on how much time you have at your disposition. Meditation should be a pleasurable spiritual exercise, not an obligation.

Each time that you decide to meditate, sit on the floor in a quiet room, close your eyes, and begin to breathe deeply. When you have attained a state of calmness and are deeply relaxed, choose a rune, hold it in your hand, and try to "sense" it. Concentrate and feel the weight of the rune and the material of which it is made. If you are able, try to sync with its energy. Keep breathing deeply and open your eyes. Place the rune on the floor in front of you. Observe the glyph that appears on the rune. What does it look like? What comes to mind?

I recall the first time I practiced this meditation. I chose Dagaz. Looking at the glyph that appeared, I thought of a butterfly. I began to visualize this small insect, observing its beauty and sense of freedom. I could see it flitting from flower to flower and moving its iridescent wings in the light of a spring morning. It was an amazing session at the end of which I felt reborn and lighter, just like a butterfly!

Targeted Meditation

Targeted meditation is focused on a problem we wish to resolve or a precise question we have formulated and which is particularly important to us. Proceed as follows:

Focusing

Sit on the ground in a comfortable position, close your eyes, and breathe deeply. Try to empty your mind. Begin to focus on the question that you want to meditate on. For example, imagine you have an important job interview. Begin to visualize the job interview, imagining the situation and how you would like it to proceed. Try to perceive the feelings connected to the situation. What do you feel? Agitation? Fear of not having the right qualifications? Once you are conscious of these feelings, choose a rune.

Formulation

Tip the bag of runes onto the ground in front of you and choose a rune that has some quality associated with the feelings that have emerged. Naturally, there will be many different runes that can be applicable to your situation: choose the one that you are most comfortable. For example, in the case cited above, I would choose Hagalaz, which contains the key words "concentration" and "self-expression," two important characteristics to have for a good interview. Now the moment has come to meditate on the characteristics of the chosen rune and absorb their energy by concentrating and opening your heart to them.

Active Meditation

After years of experience, I have discovered that the best way to meditate consists of applying the meanings of each rune and its energy to my day-to-day experiences. Instead of limiting myself to thinking passively about the rune, I try to exploit its qualities to improve the quality of my life and my relationships with others. For example, let's say that at the start of the day I extract the rune Isa from the bag. Looking at the list of questions associated with this rune, I am struck by this one: "Are we afraid of being judged by others?"

Immediately my boss comes to mind. He's a capable man, but at times, a bit sarcastic. I then try to analyze the relationship I have with him. What feelings does he provoke in me? Am I afraid of being judged by him? After this brief reflection, I look at the key words for this rune and from them I choose "self-control" and I associate these words with my boss. The rune clarifies what I need to do: try to keep my feelings of inferiority and my tendency to judge at bay.

I assure you that active meditation, a great way for harmonizing with the energies of the day, does miracles. It creates wellbeing, self-knowledge, makes us better people, and gives us the ability to create wellbeing in our own surroundings.

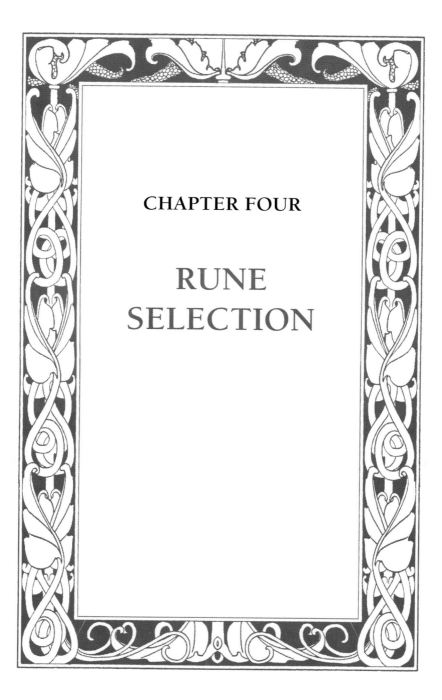

CHAPTER FOUR

RUNE
SELECTION

The time has come to think about rune selection. The symbols that appear on the runes are always the same, but the materials used to create the runes and the way this material harmonizes with surrounding energies can change many things.

As you become more experienced in working with the runes, you may feel the need to have and use many different sets of runes. Don't limit yourself, as this is a natural progression. At the same time, if you wish to give the runes as a gift to someone, try to find a type of rune that is suitable to their needs and personality.

There are many types of runes available for purchase, comprised of various materials and available in different colors. One summer I made my own runes by choosing twenty-five small white stones from a beach and drew the corresponding symbols on them.

In general, three types of materials used for making runes: wood, stone, and crystal.

STONE AND CRYSTAL

The difference between stone and crystal is very simple. Crystal (rose quartz, amethyst, rock crystal) has a strongly homogeneous structure, which means that the same molecule structure is repeated over and over. This ordered structure gives it its characteristic luminosity. Stone (black agate, rose cornel, bloodstone) is an inhomogeneous conglomerate of molecules that are identical but of diverse structure, characterized often by an opaque color. According to crystal therapy, stone and crystal act very differently on an energy level.

RUNES ADAPTED TO PERSONALITY

How then does one select the runes that are most suitable to one's personality? This section answers this question by looking at the properties of the materials and the colors that can be found in runes available today.

Each color and material has a different property and bring with them different energies. Once specifically analyzed, choosing the best runes for your needs becomes child's play! Prior to examining the materials and colors, I wish to give you some general advice.

Take your time, choose the moment

As you learn to use the runes, they will become an intimate presence in your daily life. For this reason, take your time and do not hurry in making your selection. Before purchasing your runes, spend a few days imagining them by using a technique called free association. What color would you give to your personality? What color would you associate with the present moment? What do you think your soul feels like? Is it hot or cold? Smooth or rough? These questions are obviously just suggestions, so feel free to use them or formulate your own questions.

One last piece of advice I have for you is to write the answers to these questions in a small notebook. It's a good idea to keep a small notebook that you can use to document your journey and experiences with the runes, from the moment you choose them onwards.

Listen to your eyes, hands, and your heart

When the time has arrived to purchase the runes, ask the shopkeeper if you can look, touch, and hold their weight in your hands. I realize this is not always possible, especially if you buy them online. Pay attention to the colors that you are drawn to.

Do not underestimate the importance of weight or the sensations you feel as you touch the different materials. Once you have taken these things into account, keep in mind that the most important thing is to find runes that capture your heart.

A doubt to resolve

It is possible that you will be unable to decide between two types of runes that particularly attract your attention. Which ones should you choose? Naturally you can use more than one type of rune, but if cost is an issue, you could begin with the purchase of one type, deciding to add to your collection at a later date.

Having now given you these preliminary tips and having eliminated any doubts that may have arisen during the selection process, I can now begin to talk about the different materials and colors of runes.

THE MATERIALS USED TO CREATE THE RUNES

Take a piece of wood, a stone, and a crystal and place them in some light. The wood will absorb it, the stone will reflect it, and it will pass through the crystal. Move them close to a flame. The wood will burn while the stone and the crystal will become hot. Place them in water. The stone and the wood change color but the crystal does not. These materials are alive. They react to stimuli just like we do.

When we interact with these diverse materials, we forge a unique link with them. We can be allergic to certain materials or feel a particular sense of well-being when in contact with others.

In different cultures, certain materials are seen as symbols of strength and power, such as gold, silver, and precious stones. Over the centuries, the runes have been incised on many different materials, with the most ancient archeological findings being made of metal. The runes have also been inscribed onto terracotta and hung on the outside of houses as a sign of good luck. It is still possible to find enormous runic stones in Scandinavia today.

When we choose to use the runes as an oracle, not only do we need to pay attention to the materials they have been made with, but we must also keep in mind that its energetic characteristics need to be in harmony with our own.

WOODEN RUNES

Wood is considered a warm material. It grows and develops in the ground, needs water and sunlight, and it breathes. Therefore the four elements are present in wood: air, water, earth and fire.

Temperament: Wooden runes are suitable for people who are very cerebral and who find it difficult to find serenity in everyday life. Wood can help them to balance these characteristics and to resolve situations by looking at the concrete side of things with a touch of common sense. Wood guides people to stay grounded, just like trees and bushes have strong roots from which they get their life.

These runes are also recommended for people who have trouble expressing their emotions. Wood can help them to "warm" their hearts and to communicate with others. Wood is a sensual material, very pleasing to touch and is recommended to those who wish to explore their sexuality and all that is connected with the body and its pleasures on a deeper level.

Situations: Wood runes are useful for when we want to shed light on practical problems in our life or give precedence to the practical sides of a multi-faceted problem. Wood is particularly suited to situations regarding the home, the workplace, or relationships with partners or family, all of which will be illuminated by the warm and positive energy of wood. Even financial problems can be understood with more wisdom and precision. Furthermore, wooden runes are suitable in resolving doubts that concern children, animals, plants, and other things that need to be taken care of.

Energy: The energy of wood brings wellness to the heart, regenerates the body, and is perfect for helping those who have recovered from an illness of some type. It protects pregnant women and helps those who wish to conceive. It protects the home, the family, one's environment, and brings forth serenity and calm. It is useful for those undertaking a new initiative of a commercial type and for those who work for themselves.

STONE RUNES

Every stone has its own story connected to its color, luminosity, weight, and the feeling of energy we get from it simply holding it in our hands.

Temperament: Stone runes hold great creative potential and for this reason are appropriate for those of an artistic temperament. These aspects are amplified and stimulated by the specific energies of individual stones. Stone is suitable for very exuberant people as it has the power to channel energies into constructive actions. Personalities that tend towards melancholy or pessimism get a positive lashing from stone, while those individuals who embrace the pleasures of life will be rebalanced by stone runes. This rebalancing will not take away their joy of life but will aid them in resisting excesses and viewing reality with clarity and rationally. Stone runes are very good for those who work with the body, either their own or others. Stone also has a stabilizing power and is appropriate for people who are insecure or who often fall prey to instincts and impulses.

Situations: Runes made from stone are suitable for exploring the link between people and the environment that surrounds them. Do we have trouble channeling our energies and expressing ourselves profoundly? We can ask stone runes for help. Situations that regard self-expression, self-esteem, and authority are efficiently investigated via stone runes. In addition, stone runes are suitable for questions that involve love and emotions and for situations that require rapid and efficacious action and a certain sense of self-assuredness when making a choice.

Energy: Stone reacts to our self-esteem. It stimulates optimism and serenity and provides us with a good dose of realism, which is indispensable in realizing our dreams. It increases creativity and the need for self-affirmation. It favors sentimental ties and aids those in search of their soul mate.

CRYSTAL RUNES

Crystals possess a powerful creative energy. They are always associated with purity for their beauty alone and for this reason are considered a source of healing and symbolize rebirth.

Temperament: Crystal runes are suitable for people who are undertaking a spiritual journey and for those who wish to further their experience in the field of meditation. Each crystal has naturally diverse characteristics, but in general this type of rune acts on the spirituality of a person and on their inner knowledge.

These runes are suitable for people who wish to undertake or are already dedicated to the study of esoteric disciplines and for those who wish to explore the more hidden or subtle side of a problem.

They are appropriate for people who search for solitude and knowledge during certain periods of their life; to people who feel free and nomadic; and to women who wish to go beyond the role traditional society has imposed on them. Crystal runes can also be useful to teachers, therapists, or to anyone who works with others in pursuits of knowledge.

Situations: Runes made from crystal are ideal for resolving problems, doubts, or questions regarding our spirituality. Crystal runes also have a strong connection to karma and can answer questions or resolve problems connected to the past, our ancestors, and our genealogy. Crystal runes can provide answers regarding existential questions or our motivations, and can ease our doubts regarding our roles in life. Even highly abstract questions are suitable for analyzing with these runes.

Energy: Crystal is better able to receive, accumulate, transmit, and transport energy than wood or stone. This applies to energy connected to people as well as energy connected to the environment. Crystal runes favor concentration and self-knowledge. They give the gift of empathy toward others and the ability to find original and efficient solutions to all kinds of problems. They protect those who have to face exams or studies. They enable moments of solitude to be fruitful, creative, and regenerative. Furthermore, crystal runes are helpful to those who are experiencing stress and to those who have heavy mental workloads.

THE COLORS OF THE RUNES

Colors have the ability to stimulate the subconscious in a subtle way. Some psychological studies have demonstrated that certain colors favor particular states of mind and thoughts, and therefore act on our way of being.

The colors of runes that are available today are many, with some runes being multi-colored (the properties of the stones with mixed colors can be understood by looking at the diverse colors they are comprised of and following the indications dedicated to mixed color runes). The choice of color for the runes is very important, as each one will stimulate certain thoughts and behaviors.

below: Runes of different colors and materials: Green aventurine, rose quartz and red jasper

We can use the colors of the runes by analyzing them on three different levels: contemplative, for meditation; active, to enhance certain characteristics in ourselves; and magical, to protect us in certain situation.

Contemplative, for meditation

Get comfortable in a quiet room and throw the runes onto a cloth. While taking a few deep, relaxing, and profound breaths, delve into the color, letting it illuminate and lull you with the images and thoughts that the vibrations of the color suggest to you.

Active, to enhance certain characteristics in ourselves

Stare at the runes, paying attention to the emotions that you feel. Don't judge them by moral parameters (don't worry if your feelings are positive or negative); concentrate instead on their essence and power.

Magical, to protect us in certain situations

Select one rune in a color that you like and place it in your pocket or bag. Use it as protection in specific predicaments and as a way of helping you to develop or enhance certain characteristics of your personality.

We will now examine the colors in detail, beginning with the primary colors (red, blue, yellow) and moving successively onto the derived colors (green, orange, purple, white, black, gray, and brown).

RED

Energetic and stimulating, red is associated with fire. It is heat, life and blood, courage, passion, confusion and anger.

Personality: Those who choose runes of a red color are optimistic, decisive, impulsive, combative, competitive, passionate, enthusiastic, an extrovert, and autonomous. They look for prestige, feeling a need to dominate and to affirm themselves professionally. They have a very vivacious temperament, with a great desire to act. This is a courageous individual who tries to fully live every moment and does everything possible for affirmation, always looking for a place in the foreground. They make decisions without hesitating and work with vigor and power. They have a practical intelligence and a spirit of sacrifice.

Contemplative level: As the color red is the color of fire, of blood, of vital charges, and of actions, this will be a guide in meditations on situations that need strong decisions and the ability to resolve conflicts. The images suggested and invoked by red runes are those of fire and of lava that descends; of workshops where metal is forged; of indoor fireplaces where a happy family spends its time together.

Active level: Red stimulates courage, instincts, passion. It is therefore suitable for people who have difficulty getting in touch with their feelings and that experience times in their lives where they have little faith and self-esteem and have difficulty making decisions.

Magical level: Red runes provide protection from accidents and potentially dangerous situations. They keep dishonest and violent people away. They nurture relationships with the opposite sex and give the gift of charisma and charm.

Red stones: red cornel, red onyx, red jasper
Red crystals: ruby, garnet, tourmaline

BLUE

Blue encourages mental and emotional serenity. It is connected to gifts of reliability and indicates religious and spiritual tendencies.

Personality: Those who choose blue runes have a sweet and gentle nature. They are soft and romantic, simple and sensible. They love nature, animals, and children. They have a great spirit, good faith, ingenuity, and dedication. In general, they have a youthful appearance and emanate a strong sense of calm. They appreciate sincerity and honesty and look for cordial and enduring relationships. They love to study, to reflect, and are attracted to mystery. They are capable of communicating very well and express themselves with great ease. They are faithful and trustworthy. They are good at intellectual pursuits. Furthermore, they are great company, understanding and tolerant, affectionate, and not at all jealous.

Contemplative level: Blue is the color of the sea, sky, tranquility, tenderness, the joy of living, and is perfect for meditating on spiritual or emotional questions. As it is linked to serenity and clarity, it is suitable for illuminating particularly complex situations. Blue evokes the following images: the sea, lakes, streams, the sky, a field of cornflowers, and the cape of the Madonna.

Active level: Blue stimulates tranquility, peace, mildness, and trust in oneself and one's own strengths. It is appropriate for people who frequently live in a state of agitation and are not at peace with their own feelings or those of others. Blue runes are strong harmonizers in family life.

Magical level: Blue runes protect in situations where there is the need to maintain calm. They encourage travel and make trips pleasurable (especially in a boat or in an airplane).

Blue stones: blue onyx, lapis lazuli, blue sodalite, blue calcite, blue agate, turquoise

Blue crystals: Sapphire, blue tourmaline, blue quartz, aquamarine

YELLOW

This color denotes mental clarity and intellectual maturity. It stimulates thought processes, reanimates the spirit, and eliminates fear.

Personality: Those who choose yellow runes have an open character and are optimistic, extroverted, funny and mischievous, calm and cordial. They are enthusiastic about life and get excited easily. They care a lot about affirming themselves and attaining positions of personal prestige. They are always in search of new experiences, are optimistic, and desire a full and intense life. They are very convincing, ambitious, vain, and courageous, but are also generous. They need to feel important. Yellow also represents intelligence, wisdom, language—gifts that those who choose yellow possess.

Contemplative level: Yellow is the color of the sun, gold, happiness, lightheartedness, and fantasy. It is hot, cheerful, restorative, dynamic, and creative. It is appropriate for inquiring and meditating on in situations where spiritual matters are in discussion, or on questions of leadership and one's authority over others. It is also suitable for resolving problems and questions regarding vitality and one's physical state. Images linked to these runes are the sun, mimosa, the yolk of an egg, and bile.

Active level: Yellow stimulates optimism, vitality, and is efficacious for communicating one's ideas. It is an extroverted color, and therefore useful in group activities. Its energies flow towards the outside, to creativity and to play. It is very useful for shy and introverted people who have difficulty interacting with others.

Magical level: Yellow runes protect children and artists. They are useful in all group situations and in those involving play, such as school trips or holidays. Yellow runes make contact with nature even more pleasurable.

Yellow stones: pyrite, yellow jasper
Yellow crystals: golden quartz, topaz, citrine, yellow fluorite

GREEN

This color has a harmonizing, calming, and restorative influence. It is the color of nature and indicates fertility and prosperity, but can also indicate things that are immature and without experience.

Personality: Those who choose green-colored runes are calm and tranquil people, lovers of stability and a life without shakeups or unexpected events. These people are very honest, fair, and realistic, wanting security and continuity in their lives. They are competitive and can be social climbers. Sometimes they have difficulty collaborating with others and don't hold back from aiming for a kind of personal claim. Once an objective has been formulated, they will follow it to its conclusion with determination, drive, and mental agility. They are very efficient and capable at work, while at home they love order and cleanliness. They are also intellectuals of great morality and common sense.

Contemplative level: Green is the color of hope, of those who seek growth, and those wanting to establish themselves and to command.

It is particularly suitable for questions concerning the future and one's capabilities. Questions about family or births will also be illuminated by energy from green-colored runes. Furthermore, green helps to meditate on the reasons for one's creativity. The images that these runes evoke are trees, lawns, leaves, grasshoppers, and apples.

Active level: Green is appropriate for young people and those seeking their own accomplishments. It is also suitable for those people, regardless of age, who are seeking balance for themselves. Green is a color associated with fertility and is suitable for women who wish to become pregnant.

Magical level: Green runes protect all projects in their first phases of development. They stimulate the capacity to be enterprising and are suitable for all things new. Green runes are also good talismans for those working with nature.

Green stones: green malachite, aventurine, jade, crisopazio, green calcite, blood stones
Green crystals: emeralds, green quartz, paraiba tourmaline

ORANGE

The color orange is slightly stimulating and gives energy, but not as strongly as red. Orange relieves anxiety and worries, stimulates mental alertness, and favors physical vitality.

Personality: Those who choose orange runes are by nature happy and lively. Their behavior in general is brilliant, positive, and energetic. Those who prefer orange have a simple way of reasoning, which is clear and linear as well as very coherent and friendly. They are usually talkative, extroverted, and sociable. They fully appreciate life, expressing courage everywhere and always, and are spontaneous and good-humored. Their relationships with others are optimal. They respect everyone and have a great sense of humanity. They have a need to experience new things and to be involved in diverse projects.

Contemplative level: Orange is the color of optimism and excess. It is the color of sincere and open people, and it is the color that tends toward the practical side of life. For this reason, it is perfect for questions that regard the concrete and financial sphere. Orange is also good for any problems or questions that are concerned with the practical organization of work and daily routine due to its energy and vigor. Images connected to it are the orange, sunset, tulips, autumnal leaves, and carrots.

Active level: Orange stimulates optimism and vitality. It is suitable for people who are of a serious and melancholy disposition, as it will give them a lashing of cheerfulness. Those who are undecided and are afraid of making a wrong decision will benefit from the energy and enthusiasm transmitted by the color orange.

Magical level: Orange-colored runes protect sporting and financial undertakings. They encourage serenity and high spirits within in the family, with friends, and in couples. They favor an optimistic view in day-to-day life.

Orange stones: amber, orange agate, red cornel
Orange crystals: orange quartz, topaz

PURPLE

The color purple, by stabilizing mental readiness, stimulates creative energy and sharpens sensitivity. At times, however, it can provoke depression in very sensitive souls. It is associated with wealth, royalty, social status, spirituality, and faith in oneself.

Personality: Those who choose runes of this color tend to have a rather difficult character with a tendency to be contrary and irreconcilable. They need to feel free. They want to charm and provoke sympathy and admiration wherever they go. They are very willing and communicative, are very humane, cultivate interests at a high level, and are refined and sensitive. They wish to help others in a significant way and have inclinations toward the occult, magic, and the mysterious. They have good taste and look after themselves. They are cultured in the arts and beauty and love an exciting lifestyle.

Contemplative level: Purple is the color of the arts, of fantasy, of dreams, altruism, and healing. It represents dignity and nobility, intelligence, prudence, humility, and wisdom. Purple is a spiritual color and is suitable for use in meditation by those who are attracted to disciplines such as martial arts or yoga. It is the color of intelligence and of abstraction, and is therefore useful in questions regarding complex thought processes. The images that this color invokes are fields of lavender, bunches of grapes, wisteria, and the light of dawn on the sea.

Active level: Purple stimulates thought, abstraction, a love of beauty, and independence. It is useful for people who have dependency problems, as it increases autonomy. It is not suitable for those who suffer from depression; however, those who are very impulsive will benefit from its calming vibrations.

Magical level: Purple runes protect those who practice meditation and who are undertaking studies in disciplines such as the occult, psychology, or astrology. It is a color suitable for therapists and teachers as it favors didactics and the art of teaching in a clear and altruistic manner.

Purple stones: Korean jade, purple magnetite
Purple crystals: amethysts, purple quartz, purple tourmaline, fluorite

WHITE

This color is connected to the positive polarity present in all aspects of life—the white that indicates purity, sanity, and unconditional love. It not only reflects all colors but is also the color from which all other colors are born.

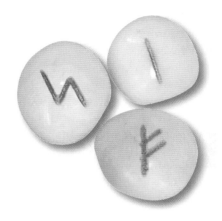

Personality: Those who choose white runes have a natural aptitude for taking care of others and possess a maternal spirit. They are people with an extremely delicate and kind soul who dedicate themselves to others with real altruism and generosity. They appreciate the hidden qualities in those who they come in contact with and know how to value them. For this reason, they are optimal teachers or therapists. Their spirit is noble and their behavior is pure and impartial. They don't care to be in the limelight but can quickly become a point of reference for others. They have notable leadership qualities that they exert in the best manner. They do not tolerate arrogance or pettiness.

Contemplative level: As white is the color of purity and of rebirth, it is suitable for questions that regard children (both those you have and those you wish to have), homes, and emotions. White is pure light and for this reason has an enormous healing power. It is perfect for meditations that concern health or during periods of convalescence. Images associate with this color are the snow, clouds, egg whites, marble, sea foam, and milk.

Active level: White stimulates compassion, brotherhood, empathy, and universal love. It is the color of joy and of the moon. For this reason it is very useful to people who experience moments of sadness and solitude. The vibrations of this color recharge those who are under stress.

Magical level: White runes protect against illness and provide strength in times of solitude. They are appropriate for purifying the atmosphere and attract people to us that are upstanding and honest.

White stones: white onyx, white agate
White crystals: white quartz

BLACK

Black is connected to the polar negativity present in all aspects of life. Black is darkness, the absence of light. It encloses within itself all colors and represents the obscure womb of life, from which all creatures are born and to which they return.

Personality: Those who choose black runes have a powerful and charismatic personality. Their thoughts are serious and profound. They love investigating the mysterious and all that is unclear. They hold unshakeable feelings and are very devout, but they can also be excessively jealous and possessive and are not always faithful. Their spirit is agitated by an incessant desire for advancement in all areas. They are very ambitious people and often attain what they want by using rather unorthodox methods. They are attracted to magic and are very sensitive, intuitive, and can sense the emotional currents around them with extraordinary precision.

Contemplative level: Black is the color of darkness and of the night. It recalls all that is mysterious and enigmatic. Its vibrations are suitable for meditating on the unknown and all that we fear. Runes of this color are excellent for clarifying the conscious and unconscious influences of energies and power. The images that this color evokes are the night, the darkness, smoke, a wolf's fur, and carbon.

Active level: Black stimulates intelligence, ambition, deep thoughts, and feelings. It is a very powerful color and is appropriate for people who nurture doubts about their charisma and for those who want to increase their sexual potency. Furthermore, black runes are suitable for people who have difficulty speaking in public.

Magical level: Black runes protect from deceits, gossip, and legal problems. They favor control over situations and give great acumen and the capacity to turn events in one's favor.

Black stones: black agate, black malachite, obsidian
Black crystals: black tourmaline, black quartz

GRAY

A union of black and white, gray is associated with neutrality, maturity, wisdom, and superior intelligence.

Personality: Those who choose gray runes posses a multifaceted personality with many characteristics, some of which may contradict themselves: uncertainty, purity, frankness, sensitivity, timidity, and a lack of self-esteem. Their intelligence is notable but they are often inflexible and tend to be very judgmental. They are solitary people who tend to distance themselves from situations, and can even be a bit introverted. They may appear cold, unapproachable, and unfriendly. They are scared to face life. They worry about things happening and about other external influences. They detest compromise and don't let themselves become involved. They love the truth and are full of hope.

Contemplative level: Gray is the color of fog, shadows and cracks, and elegance and distinction. It is appropriate for meditating on both mental and emotional questions, where clarity of thought as well as lucid distancing and a clear and precise view of all aspects of the problem are necessary. The vibrations from the color gray are optimal for analyzing complex judicial problems, such as divorce, where various aspects of reality intersect and reasons and interests from more than one side converge. Gray is also suitable for contemplating questions about our own past. The images associated with this color are stones, smoke, fog, rain-filled clouds, a winter sky, and cement.

Active level: Gray stimulates concentration and separation. It is appropriate for those who need to face an important test in their studies and those who have trouble committing to an activity in a constant and continuous manner. The vibrations from gray relax and cool passions, so therefore are also suitable for those who are experiencing emotional pain due to an amorous misadventure.

Magical level: Gray runes give longevity and are suitable for older people or those with a few aches and pains. These runes provide protection in exams, in work interviews, in business dealings, and in financial transactions.

Gray stones: hematite
Gray crystals: fluorite, gray tourmaline, smoky-gray quartz

BROWN

Brown can be seen as a variant of orange, though it is less energetic and more concrete. It indicates materiality, roots in the ground, reliability, and solidity.

Personality: Those who choose brown runes are people who can be trusted, who are calm, reflective, passive, and integral. From an emotional perspective, they need a stable and secure relationship and look for a partner who loves the same things as they do. They very much desire the peace and stability of a home. They have a simple and linear character, possess a great strength of spirit, believe in traditions, and do not like new things very much. They possess concentration, perseverance, logic, an inner richness, and a great capacity for work.

Contemplative level: Brown is the color of the earth, the trunks of the trees, of security, of love for one's origins, prudence, patience, and tenacity. It is suitable for questions about one's family and the relationships that connect various components of this family. Brown also highlights meditations about friendship and what bonds one person to another in a very effective way. This rune is also optimal for questions concerning money. Images associated with brown are the earth, the bark of trees, and wood.

Active level: Brown stimulates the strength of will, trust in oneself, and inner stability. It is favorable to those who are apart from their families, as it will make them nevertheless feel loved and connected. These runes are also appropriate for those who have difficulty feeling good about their own bodies.

Magical level: Brown runes protect the family, couples, the home, and one's patrimony. They favor relationships with others and business trips.

Brown stones: brown jasper, amber, fossil wood, tiger's eyes
Brown crystals: topaz, brown quartz

ROSE

The color rose is traditionally linked to the heart and to emotions. It stimulates harmony of the emotions and the intellect, generates optimism, and softens conflicts. Unfortunately it is not suitable for dreamers, as it risks making them live in a fantastic but unreal world.

RUNE SELECTION

Personality: Those who choose rose-colored runes have a sweet and remissive character, a great need for others, and a need to feel accepted. The greatest gift it brings is fantasy and a penchant to possess an optimistic view, even though care must be taken to not live too much in a dream world. These individuals are artists who have the potential to use their great imaginations for the good of humanity. They are good friends who know how to listen and to advise others with tenderness and empathy, as well as being capable of finding original solutions. The danger of such personalities is in a certain tendency towards laziness and superficiality, as well as a certain ingenuity that leads them to trust indiscriminately.

Contemplative level: Rose is the color of tenderness and of optimism, goodness, and happiness. It represents nobility of the spirit, intelligence of the heart, a mild temperament, and an eternally youthful spirit. This is a relaxing color and can be adapted for meditation for those who are victims of stress and pessimism as well as for those who have trouble taking time for themselves. Thanks to its character, rose is also suitable for meditations on questions that regard emotional and sentimental problems or interpersonal relationships. Images that rose evokes are rosettes, the heart, the aurora, flowering cherry trees, and sugared almonds.

Active level: Rose stimulates optimism, fantasy, daydreaming, happiness, and fun. It is useful for people who are excessively serious and who have difficulty letting go and enjoying the playful side of life. It is also suitable for those who work with children or animals. Rose stimulates empathy and compassion for the smallest and weakest individuals.

Magical level: Rose-colored runes protect those who work with feelings and emotions: therapists, artists, teachers. It is a color that is appropriate for those who, in some way, have power over others as it helps them to use their power in an ethical and non-manipulative way.

Rose stones: rose calcite
Rose crystals: rose quartz

TRANSPARENT/CLEAR

Transparency denotes innocence and purity of the soul. It stimulates trust in life, restarts empathy, and eliminates negative thoughts.

Personality: Those who choose transparent or clear runes have a sweet and reflective character. They are curious and trusting, and approach life with a purity that could become excessive. They love abstract thought and never stop at the surface of things. They want to deeply feel the experiences they live. Even though they are friendly and kind, they do not fear solitude. In fact, they need it. They possess great tact and have a particular harmony with animals and nature. A transparent color also represents mental sharpness, clairvoyance, and compassion for humanity, candor, and a goodness of the spirit.

Contemplative level: Transparency is the color of water. It represents a pure spirit, one who can be "read," a person who is not afraid of their own feelings. It is suitable for inquiring into everything regarding the emotions and can even be used for questions connected to karma and life after death. People attracted to transparent or clear runes have a great spirit and are much evolved. They are able to help others with their psychological and existential problems. Images connected to these runes include ice, crystal, water, and glass.

Active level: Transparent or clear runes stimulate study, concentration on metaphysical and abstract problems, and compassion towards others. It is a color of reflection and is useful in everything relating to the mind. Its energies go inward to emotions and dreams. It is very useful to people who have difficulty concentrating and who begin lots of different activities without bringing any of them to fruition.

Magical level: Transparent runes protect those who study, such as psychologists, and those on spiritual quests. They are useful in all situations that require concentration regarding a problem and in moments of meditation. They make spiritual activities particularly rewarding.

Transparent or clear stones: non-existent
Transparent or clear crystals: diamonds, zircon, rock crystal

MULTI-COLORED RUNES

Multi-colored runes, regardless of the colors they are composed of, bring happiness and lightness. They help us to look at life optimistically and not take it too severely.

Personality: Those who choose runes of mixed colors have an unpredictable and changing nature. They love risk and adventure and can't stand routine. They possess a sort of third eye and look at the world from a particular viewpoint. Their way of reasoning is never banal, but at times it can be a bit contorted, as these people have trouble being concise. They are generous individuals with a thousand different interests. They begin many things and have an innate capacity to rally people together. Chatting with them is a very pleasant and happy experience, as they are uninhibited and often comical. They are volcanoes of ideas and just need to focus their concentration in order to realize some of them.

Contemplative level: Multi-colored runes represent originality and the endless facets of reality. For this reason they are suitable for situations that need to remain fluid. They are optimal runes for shining light on sentimental problems where one needs to let go and remember the eternal intermittency of the heart and where judgment needs to be suspended.

Images associated with multi-colored runes are leopard skin, autumnal leaves of many hues, and sunsets with a variegation of clouds that appear like confetti.

Active level: Multi-colored runes stimulate movement and promote anti-conformism. They are suitable for people who are a little rigid and moralistic: they give them a bit of lightness and happiness. They stimulate the desire to travel and to discover things from a totally new point of view.

Magical level: Multi-colored runes protect during long trips and in tormented love affairs. They help the user to develop a sense of humor and irony, enabling problems to be faced with optimism.

Multi-colored stones: tiger's eyes, agate, travertine
Multi-colored crystals: quartz, mixed tourmaline

PURCHASING RUNES

This list does not represent all the runes currently available on the market. However, I thought it would be useful to provide a brief list of the properties of more common or beautiful types of runes.

Runes in Wood
wood: strength, substantiality, resistance

Runes in Stone
black agate: regeneration, trust, concentration
aventurine: growth, renewal, creativity
rose cornel: energy, courage, loyalty
rose jasper: protection, practicality, instinct
hematite: vigor, charisma, willpower
white onyx: talent, purity, transformation
blue onyx: calmness, inner peace, clairvoyance
bloodstone: vitality, optimism, enthusiasm

Runes in Crystal
amethyst: purification, lucidity, knowledge
rock crystal: equilibrium, wisdom, evolution
golden quartz: wellbeing, positivity, spiritual reawakening
rose quartz: harmony, serenity, self-realization

We have finally arrived at the end of this book. Now the real journey begins, the one that will enable you to find happiness within yourselves, starting with the runes. It will be an adventurous and stimulating voyage. Some of you will feel tired and defeated; others will be overflowing with joy and gratitude, incredulous for the treasures that you will discover within your own souls. Runes liberate great and powerful energies within us, and your job is to use these energies to arrive ever more deeply at the roots of realities.

Before I say goodbye, I wish to give you all a final gift: my interpretation of the rune I selected immediately after I had finished writing this volume. The rune was Hagalaz, one of my favorites. It instructs us to never be afraid of our emotions or our untamed sides and indicates a force that we can learn to control.

What wish could be better?

Bianca Luna

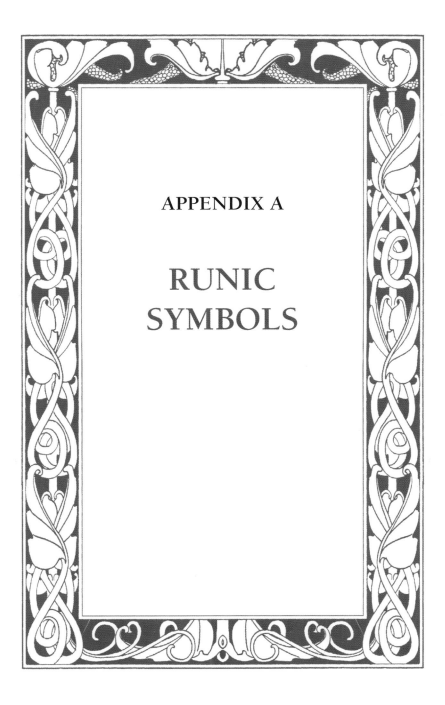

APPENDIX A

RUNIC
SYMBOLS

1. Fehu 2. Uruz 3. Thurisaz

4. Ansuz 5. Raidho 6. Kenaz

7. Gebo 8. Wunjo 9. Hagalaz

10. Nauthiz 11. Isa 12. Jera

13. Eihwaz   14. Perdho   15. Algiz

16. Suwilo   17. Tiwaz   18. Berkana

19. Ehwaz   20. Mannaz   21. Laguz

22. Inguz   23. Othala   24. Dagaz

APPENDIX B

RUNES
AVAILABLE
FOR SALE

www.llewellyn.com

Black Agate Runes

Rose Quartz Runes

Amethyst Runes

RUNES AVAILABLE FOR SALE

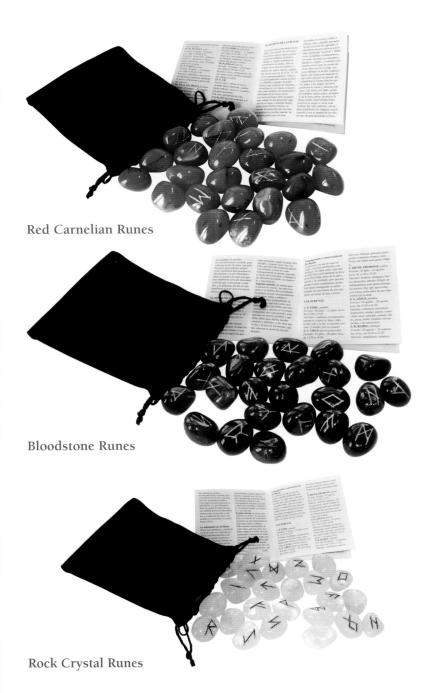

Red Carnelian Runes

Bloodstone Runes

Rock Crystal Runes

Green Aventurine Runes

Red Jasper Runes

White Onyx Runes

RUNES AVAILABLE FOR SALE